JOHN NEWTON

JOHN NEWTON

John Crotts

PUBLISHING WITH A MISSION

EP BOOKS
Faverdale North,
Darlington, DL3 0PH, England

sales@epbooks.org
www.epbooks.org

EP Books are distributed in the USA by:
JPL Distribution
3741 Linden Avenue Southeast
Grand Rapids, MI 49548

E-mail: orders@jpldistribution.com
Tel: 877.683.6935

First published 2013

British Library Cataloguing in Publication Data available
ISBN: 978-0-85234-908-3

CONTENTS

TIMELINE

24 July 1725	John Newton is born to John and Elizabeth in Wapping
11 July 1732	John's mother Elizabeth dies
December 1742	John meets Polly for the first time
March 1744	John is impressed into the navy
1745–1747	John is enslaved off the coast of West Africa
10 March 1748	The massive storm at sea begins John's spiritual awakening
1 February 1750	John marries Polly
1750–1754	John makes three voyages as slave-ship captain

May 1754	John meets spiritual friend Captain Alexander Clunie at St Kitts
August 1755	John begins job as Surveyor of the Tides in Liverpool
August 1758	John prays about entering the ministry
April, June 1764	John is ordained first as deacon and then priest for St Peter's and St Paul's Church, Olney
14 September 1767	William Cowper moves to Olney
1779	*Olney Hymns* published
8 December 1779	John becomes rector of St Mary Woolnoth, London
1780	*Cardiphonia* published
15 December 1790	Polly dies
May 1800	John preaches a funeral sermon for William Cowper
21 December 1807	John dies and is buried at St Mary Woolnoth
25 January 1893	John and Polly's remains are reinterred at Olney because of construction of the London Underground Bank station

1

THE MAN AMAZED BY GRACE

The inspired sage wrote, 'Whoever walks with the wise becomes wise, but the companion of fools will suffer harm' (Proverbs 13:20). Solomon is saying that you become like the people with whom you hang around. Your closest friends always mentor you for better or for worse.

In addition to choosing to surround yourself with the wisest men and women you can find, you can also walk with wise men and women from other times and places by reading biographies. A godly man or woman has experienced God's Spirit leading him or her through all kinds of challenges. You can always find helpful connections to your own life while you are reading.

You will laugh with them in their triumphs and shed tears through their trials. The lessons God taught them over the years can become yours too. The best biographies draw the lessons to the surface of their pages for you to skim off the top.

Over the past few years I have become good friends with John Newton. Although he lived in a different country than I do and over 200 years before me, the Lord Jesus Christ mercifully saved him and used him to spread the message of God's mercy to others. John Newton fleshes out many lessons that I need to put into practice as a cross-centred Christian.

The people who know John Newton's name often only know one or two things about him. They recognize that he authored one of the most popular hymns of all time, 'Amazing Grace'. The other thing they sometimes know is that he was a slave-ship captain before he wrote that hymn. Those facts are true, but there is a great deal more to his story!

John Newton sailed all over the Mediterranean Sea with his sea-captain father from the time he was eleven years old. He only went to school for two years, but he taught himself Latin, French, Greek and Hebrew, and he wrote countless songs and books. At one point, he was captured and forced to join the British Navy. For two years, he was literally enslaved off the west coast of Africa before he helped to enslave others.

John's love for a girl kept him alive although she did not even know that he loved her. His conversion to Christianity happened over a span of six years. He was rejected for ordination several times before he became a minister at almost forty years old. He served as a minister in only two churches for the next forty-four years. John Newton wrote hundreds of hymns and published one of the first hymn-books in the church. The former slave and slaver played an important role in mentoring and helping William Wilberforce to abolish the slave trade in England. Newton's story is compelling for its own sake, but it is also filled with helpful instruction.

The hymn 'Amazing Grace' was written for his country congregation to go with a sermon he was going to preach, but its theme marked Newton's entire life. He never got over that fact that God saved him. His godly mother had tried to direct his young heart to love Jesus. But when she died, he rebelled against the Lord. John Newton deserved to go to hell for ever, and he knew it. When a massive storm at sea drove him to cry out for God's mercy, he really doubted whether God had enough grace for a wretch like him; but God showed John Newton favour.

The only reason God could justly forgive Newton is because the cross accomplished much more than most people realize. God let his Son die upon the cross in the place of sinners — even the worst sinners! Three days later God raised Jesus from the dead. For those who turn from their sin and trust only in what Jesus accomplished, God offers to trade all of their sins for all of Jesus' righteousness. John Newton experienced that exchange. It literally put a song in his heart that he never stopped singing!

The years of struggle, turning from his sins to Jesus, deeply impressed on Newton that God's massive grace needed to affect all of his being and all of his dealings with others. Newton's mind, will and emotions were transformed by a growing understanding of the significance of God's wonderful mercy.

A consuming burden grew within his chest to tell others about the same gift of grace given to him. Newton was thrilled to personally witness John Wesley and George Whitefield proclaim this great news in the open fields of England and in house meetings. He wanted to do the same.

He served the Lord as a pastor within his local congregation and within the Church of England, but his grace-filled heart was never contained within the walls of his denomination. He loved the gospel and throughout his life he established deep friendships with gospel men and women of all backgrounds. Secondary matters were kept secondary when the gospel of God's amazing grace was to the fore.

As Christians today, we are all too easily satisfied with a surface appreciation of God's grace to us. If you think of your sin as a small problem that God took care of long ago, your life and ministry today will never be affected and shaped by utter amazement at God's grace. Certainly we learn of this as we read the inspired pages of the Bible; but we can also learn more about this by seeing it lived out in the lives of those gripped by grace. John Newton was such a man!

2

EARLY LIFE

Wapping has long since been absorbed into London; but in the early eighteenth century, Wapping was a small but bustling port on the River Thames to the north of London. On 24 July 1725, a respected merchant captain named John (d. 1750) and his wife Elizabeth (d. 1732) had their only child in that town. He too was named John.

Elizabeth was a godly woman and a wonderful mother. Since her husband, the captain, was often away slicing the waters of the Mediterranean Sea, she strongly stamped the character of young John. She was a faithful member of David Jennings' Independent Chapel on Old Gravel Lane. Like most first-time mothers, Elizabeth was devoted to her child. She hoped to prepare him for the ministry, and took full advantage of her opportunity to pour instruction into her obviously bright son. By the time John was four, Elizabeth had taught him to read and write, and the beginnings of Latin; and she had set her son to memory work. He memorized portions of the Bible, catechism questions and answers, poems, and the brand-new hymns recently published by Isaac Watts. Isaac

Watts pastored a church only a mile away and even filled the pulpit for David Jennings on occasion.

The free and easy relationship young John Newton enjoyed with his mother stands in marked contrast with the dreadful, distant relationship he endured with his father. As soon as Captain Newton landed in Wapping after a sea voyage, he would be seen striding through the streets and into the door of his house on Red Lyon Street. Instantly, his son would change from beloved star student to scared cabin boy, as John Sr ran his home as he ran his boats. The captain demonstrated his patient love again and again in his actions for his son's benefit later on in their lives, but there was little fatherly affection flowing from the father of John Newton. Though the relationship with his son lacked warmth, Captain Newton was a capable seaman, earning respect from ship owners and fellow captains.

The godly lady who was young John's loving shelter from his stern father and the storms of life was taken from him in 1732. Elizabeth was barely thirty when she was consumed by tuberculosis. Seeking fresh air for her battered lungs, she spent her final days removed from her son in Kent in the home of her distant relatives, the Catletts.

The challenges of childhood

The turmoil swirling in John's nearly-seven-year-old heart must have spiked when his father returned home and then remarried within a space of a few weeks. The dizzy grieving boy still had his distant father, but now also a step-mother,

Thomasina, and a new place to live. His basic needs were still met, but he lost his mother's instruction and he gained more freedom to interact with profane children in the new neighbourhood. The character and content of his mother's lessons began to slip from John's bright heart and mind, as he spent more time wandering about the streets with other boys. When other half-siblings were added to his home, his parents' care for him was even more distracted.

John's only formal education in his entire life was a bad experience at a boarding school for two years in Essex during these days. These were strict and difficult days for John. The first instructor was extremely severe. John felt his young spirit being suffocated. Reading, which he had previously loved, became loathsome.

Remarkable childhood

During his childhood, John had a few amazing experiences which, many years later, he recognized as God's powerful hand preserving his life. Sometimes we benefit from such experiences at the time, but at other times we miss the point. John seems to have been the same, benefiting from some of the remarkable events while missing the significance of other events.

Once he was flung from a horse, coming within inches of a freshly-cut hedgerow with deadly stakes poking up. For a while, because of the near miss, he tried to curb the profanities he was by then using regularly with his friends, for fear of facing God's judgement. But it did not take long before he rediscovered his old vocabulary. On another occasion, he arrived a few minutes too late to join his friend and take a small boat to go on board a man-of-war. He burned in anger on the shore when he realized they had left without him. But that small boat overturned before meeting the warship, and his friend and several others drowned. When he attended the funeral of his childhood friend, he shook as he realized how easily it could have been him in the casket. Another time, looking through a religious book ignited self-made efforts at religious reformation. But the flame did not last. Some of his religious efforts during his childhood lasted longer than others, but all of them fizzled out eventually.

Four years after John's mother died, Captain Newton took his son to sea. John was only eleven years old at the time. Over the next six years, he made five Mediterranean voyages. While his father protected him somewhat from the crew, he had exacting expectations of his son. John did not grow closer to his father on these adventures, but he did learn the way of a seaman. The reputations sailors often have for saltiness proved true for those around John. The Bible says that we become like those we spend time with (Proverbs 13:20), and John's case illustrates the Bible's reliability. John's character declined to such a degree that he went from being a follower in wickedness to a leader. Foul language and foul attitudes flowed freely from John's heart and mouth.

When Captain Newton was away on trips without his son, John ran wild with the boys of his town. Although he did sprinkle in several seasons of self-reformation, they always faded into deeper expressions of his sin.

Once, at a port in Holland, he came upon a philosophical book by the liberal Lord Shaftesbury called *Characteristicks*. Although it included beautiful expressions of morality, it dislodged morality from religion. Elizabeth Newton's remaining light in her son's heart was growing dim. John later described the book as poison to his soul. He was descending from his early instruction in the Christian faith to Deism.

John meets Polly

As John was living out a life of laziness with no direction for the future, his father intervened. The captain persuaded a friend to send John to work in Jamaica and to arrange for his future provision. It was a strong employment opportunity that would be look good on Newton's CV, but it would take John overseas for four years. John agreed to take the position.

On the way to the ship, however, John decided to pay a brief visit to his distant relatives in Kent, in whose house his mother had died. After his father's remarriage, the families had drawn apart, but his father agreed to the visit, as their home was only a half-mile or so off the highway.

As John nervously approached the home, he was surprised by the visit in every way. First, the Catletts recognized him right away and welcomed him with open arms. The second surprise involved one of the Catletts' two daughters. The older daughter, Mary (or Polly, as she was called), was fourteen years old. Newton learned later that their mothers had often spoken of young John and baby Polly as potential marriage partners. Newton fell wildly in love with Polly almost instantly. In a book written nearly three hundred years after the fact, it could be tempting to overdramatize what was going on in Newton's heart. Such dramatics are hardly necessary, however, as Newton himself recorded that his love for Polly was stronger than what you read in romance novels! He had lost his religion and his morality, but over the next seven years he would never lose his affection for the young Catlett girl. Even throughout his later life he worried that his love for Polly bordered on idolatry!

Because of her age and Newton's circumstances, however, he could not let anyone know of the new fire in his heart, not even Polly. But all of his life was now seen through the prism of his affections, including the thought of spending four years on the other side of the world in Jamaica. He wilfully extended his three-day visit to three weeks! When he was sure the ship had sailed, he returned home to face the fury of his father.

Captain Newton's anger subsided sooner than expected, though, and young John was able to join the crew of a ship for a voyage to Venice. As the boat rose and sank on the sea, so also did Newton's self-made morality.

With his ship docked in the port of Venice, John experienced a remarkable dream. At the time, the dream was disturbing, but later it had special significance to him. In this dream, his night-watch was interrupted by a man who appeared on the ship's deck. The stranger offered Newton a ring to protect carefully. With this ring, the man said, he would have happiness and blessing. He went on to say that if it was lost, however, Newton would experience trouble and misery. A second man followed only to argue about the benefits of the ring. He soon shamed Newton for believing that such a gift could be so important. The man coaxed Newton into flinging the ring into the harbour where the ship was anchored. No sooner had the ring been submerged in the sea than the mountains surrounding Venice exploded into flame. As he watched the fire move through the mountains into the city, closing in on the ship, Newton's hope for the blessings of the ring were consumed. As his hope was being consumed, a third man appeared (or possibly the first man reappeared). He dived into the water and recovered the ring. The Italian fires suddenly ceased. As Newton dared to anticipate the ring being replaced, the man surprised him. He said that he would keep it for Newton, and at the time when Newton needed it, he himself would produce it for him.

Certainly, God can do whatever he will. The Bible records many dreams that God has given to people. There are also many stories of dreams, ancient and modern, in the history of the church that appear to have been divinely inspired. Still, dreamers cannot be sure of the meaning of any dream apart from the Bible. The Bible does not instruct Christians to seek dreams or tell them how to interpret them. That said, as John Newton reflected upon this particular dream, he saw a picture of salvation. The blessings of the ring are like God's blessings to an unworthy sinner, the ultimate blessing being the gift of the righteousness of Jesus Christ. Not only are rebellious creatures unworthy to receive such a gift, they cannot be trusted to maintain it either. Left to ourselves, the best person would selfishly squander and throw away all of God's blessings. The Italian fires of the dream would be engulfed by the fires of judgement they represent. The Lord Jesus, represented by the first man, not only gives us his righteousness, but he also keeps it for us in heaven. When it comes to the gift of salvation, God truly does it all. Newton's dream outside the famous city of canals seems like a glimpse of what God would do in the still-stubborn heart of this sailor. Although his dream affected him terribly, like all of his other strong impressions and even the near-death experiences during his early years, the effects were but temporary.

Forced into the navy

Whenever John Newton came back to England from his Mediterranean exploits, he always had a land journey in mind. His favourite destination was to see his Polly in Kent once again. Like others struck with lovesickness, Newton's emotions often overtook his mind. Wandering aimlessly, lost in romance, is potentially dangerous for any young person, but this was an unusually dangerous time, and Newton's case of lovesickness was unusually severe.

England's perennial enemy, France, had warships sailing uncomfortably close to British waters. England had laws to enhance the navy quickly, and in such times as these, they put laws of conscription into action. To cut through the delays of waiting for young men to volunteer for naval service or even sending draft notices to those registered with the state, England allowed press gangs to capture any young man fit for service that they could get their hands on — rather like the dog catcher rounding up the neighbourhood stray animals.

John Newton knew the dangers of the days, and he knew to
be on the alert for press gangs. But his mind was apparently
in neutral as his emotions carried him along the road from
Polly's house. Suddenly, he found himself surrounded by a
press gang and soon in a sailor suit! He had been conscripted
onto a man-of-war called *HMS Harwich*. Although his father
was a respected local captain, he was powerless to rescue his
son because of the situation with France. For the first month
John was in misery both inside and out. Eventually, Captain
Newton was able to have his son promoted to the lowest
rank of officer, a midshipman, and he was moved up to the
quarterdeck. His circumstances improved dramatically on
the outside, but he was still miserable within.

As an officer he abused his position and made life tough for
those he had once served alongside on the ship. One time
he went AWOL to see Polly for a few extra days. Although
his fellow officers successfully appealed to the captain to go
easy on the lovesick sailor, Newton's reputation never fully
recovered.

His best friend on the ship also sought to convince him to
renounce the gospel. This fellow-midshipman hammered
in the wedge that the book *Characteristicks* had become
in Newton's religion. Arguments dividing morality from
Newton's Christian upbringing effectively eroded what little
remained of his faith.

Four months after he had disappeared following his heart
to be with Polly, he sailed ashore with a group of seamen to
acquire supplies for the ship. His official job was to keep any
of them from deserting. But instead, he used the opportunity

to desert the Navy himself. He desperately tried to make his way to his father to find relief from his situation.

He walked carefully for two days, making it some twenty-five miles undetected, two hours from his father's house, before being captured by a group of soldiers. He was dragged back to Plymouth and put in chains for two days before being returned to the *Harwich*. The captain had him publicly whipped and stripped of his rank. You can imagine the delight of the men in the lower decks to have their former 'mate turned abuser' returned to their ranks. Their insults and abuse continually bit into Newton like swarming mosquitoes on a warm summer's night.

The ship's captain ordered the officers to show Newton no mercy, but some of them could not help having compassion on their utterly miserable former colleague. Only two thoughts kept Newton from taking his life: his desire to kill the captain and his love for Polly. He couldn't bear the idea that she would hear of what he had become.

A new crew

Throughout Newton's life he experienced one kind providence from God after another, many of which went ignored or unappreciated until salvation dawned in his heart. Another privilege of the eighteenth-century British Navy was the right to trade sailors with civilian ships. This gave every naval ship the opportunity to upgrade the quality of its crew by adding competent men and by subtracting its incompetents. The captain of the *Harwich* used his privilege to swap the battered and abused former midshipman, John Newton, for another man from a slave-trading ship called the *Pegasus*.

It happened like this. The *Harwich* had completed her tasks in the region and was preparing to sail to the East Indies for five long years. One fateful day as Newton overslept in his hammock, the *Harwich* encountered the *Pegasus*. While everyone else went their way, a midshipman tried to rouse the sleepy sailor. Since John would not get up, the officer cut his bed down! With his pride (and no doubt other parts of his body) bruised, John stumbled up the steps onto the deck. When he awakened to the fact that another sailor was being swapped to a ship headed for Africa, Newton came to life. He begged the lieutenants to urge the captain to dismiss him instead. Although he had refused to do so before, this time the captain took pity on Newton and allowed him to go. Within half an hour of crashing out of his severed hammock, Newton was out of the Navy and off the *Harwich*.

Life on the *Pegasus* was significantly better for Newton. The captain knew Newton's father and treated him kindly for his father's sake. But before long John's stubbornly sinful streak showed itself on his new ship. He felt nothing restraining him among these new people he did not know. Newton continually caused trouble with the crew and acted wickedly against the captain and the other officers. Not content with displaying his own sinfulness, he aggressively sought to seduce his fellow sailors into sin as well. His latent musical creativity was also put to ill use. Newton composed a song subtly insulting the captain, his leadership, and his ship. He then taught the entire crew to sing it boldly. The future hymn writer demonstrated himself in terrible ways! For some six months Newton's antics continued, and the captain lost all his initial compassion for his careless crew member.

John Newton's ship had sailed south to the west coast of Africa. Black tribal leaders within the interior of Africa captured other black men, women and children, dragged them to the coast, and sold them to European slave traders who had settled on the coast by the mouths of the rivers. When they thought that the process moved too slowly, the Europeans invaded the inland themselves to secure their human merchandise.

Slave ships generally sailed on a great triangular circuit from Europe to the west coast of Africa, then on to the Caribbean and the southern United States, and finally back across the Atlantic Ocean to their home ports. These ships brimmed with commodities from England and the other European countries to trade for the slaves in Africa. Their commodities for the middle passage were the Africans that had been enslaved. The Caribbean replaced the people with goods like sugar, rum, cotton and brandy that sold well in Europe. Until the late eighteenth century, the slave trade was viewed quite highly within British society. Of course, without modern media exposing the horrors of slavery itself, the awful conditions of the three-week middle passage, and the life of slaves in the new world, the fine opinions of the English were based on gross ignorance. As people, especially Christians, learned more of the evils of the slave trade, there swelled a movement of strong opposition.

Enslaved in Africa

John Newton himself would one day become a full captain
of a ship engaging in this horrible trade. But before he
achieved such apparent heights, he experienced virtual
African slavery himself! After reaching the coasts of Africa,
the *Pegasus* began doing its work. Newton had been on
board for about six months in total. But the captain died just
a few days before they left the coast. Newton knew he was
in trouble, as he had made quite an enemy out of the first
officer, who now assumed command. He would certainly be
placed on the first man-of-war they encountered. But instead
of waiting for a warship, Newton moved ashore, leaving the
ship to enter the service of Amos Clow, a man who had been
sailing on the ship with Newton. Clow had made a good deal
of money living on the coast of Africa buying and selling
slaves. Dreams of finding his fortune captured Newton's
mind as he left the ship with his new boss even though he
had nothing but the clothes on his back. They settled on the
Plantanes near the borders of what are now Sierra Leone
and Liberia. Their small island was only about two miles in
circumference and covered in palm trees.

Amos Clow worked the slave trade from the coast. At first
his relationship with Newton was mutually beneficial and
rewarding. They built a house and began to work. Newton
worked hard, almost trying to make up for his lost years. He
was like a partner to Clow and could foresee a long-term
relationship between the two men. Clow, however, was
living as if married to a black woman who held an influential
role within her local tribe. Her name sounded to Newton

like the letters P and I put together. Her relationship with
Clow, together with her tribal position, gave her the right to
be treated as Princess PI.

When Newton was too sick to accompany Clow on a trip up
the river to the interior, he fell into the hands of PI, who had
disliked him from the beginning. He was slow to recover,
and she made his recovery slower by her abusive treatment.
He was rarely fed and inadequately clothed. PI would also
lead the others in the household to mock and insult Newton.
Newton was so pathetic that the slaves sometimes shared
some of their meagre allotments of food with him. He was
so hungry at times that he sneaked out at night to dig up raw
roots to eat.

When Clow finally returned, things improved a little for
Newton, until he made an accusation against PI in her
presence. Clow took his wife's side of the story. On a trip
with Newton off the island, a former partner joined the
men. Perhaps motivated by a desire to prevent Newton
from getting too close to Clow, this man accused Newton
of stealing from Clow, one of the only sins of which Newton
was actually innocent during these days. Clow believed
the trader. Condemned without evidence, John Newton
became even more like a slave. He was chained to the ship's
deck when Clow and the others were onshore conducting
business. He was exposed to the full force of the elements—
brutal heat and beating wind and rain (sometimes as long as
twenty and even up to forty hours straight!), all with barely
enough clothing. He was hardly fed — one pint of rice per
day. Sometimes he was able to fish using as bait the entrails
of birds he caught. Whatever he caught he ate raw or burned

from fast broiling. This trip lasted two miserable months. When they returned to the Plantanes, his situation did not improve.

One of his few distractions during his wretched island existence was mathematics. He had a copy of *Euclid* (a geometry book) with him and, using a stick for a pen and sand for paper, he mastered the first six books! A few times during this year of virtual slavery he successfully smuggled letters to his father and Polly telling them of his situation and begging the captain to rescue him from his misery. The letters eventually made it through, and the captain called on a friend in Liverpool for help, who subsequently gave orders to one of his captains who was preparing for work in West Africa. This does not sound like the fastest or the surest rescue mission the world has ever seen!

One day as Newton was planting lemon and lime trees on the island, Clow and PI stopped their stroll to offer a bit of a sarcastic insult. Clow remarked that perhaps by the time the trees bore fruit Newton would be released and would return to the island as captain of his own ship. Although Clow was being sarcastic, his words actually proved prophetic.

A turn for the better

At last Newton was released by his master to work with another trader on the island. Almost immediately John's life took a positive turn. His new boss treated him much better than Clow and PI had. He ate well and had adequate clothing. Newton became a companion to his new boss and was entrusted with the oversight of people and goods. He was almost like a partner. The boss had a number of factories along the coastline, and Newton and a fellow servant were dispatched some hundred miles away to a place called Kittam to manage one of the businesses. They lived as they pleased and were faring very well. To Newton's mind, his African future seemed to have become a good prospect after all, perhaps even better than it could have been in England. An old African saying was becoming true of Newton; that he was a white man growing black. The African attitudes and ways of life were fitting Newton almost as well as his new clothes.

While he was at this factory along a river only a mile or so from the coast, a ship called the *Greyhound* was looking for Newton, sending out feelers for his whereabouts as it traced the coastline. Of course, Newton was not at all where he was supposed to be. The fact is that if Newton had been on the Plantanes or at any of his boss' other factories, the ship would have sailed past before John even knew that someone was looking for him. But God sent that ship to Kittam. Not only does God have a perfect map, he also has a perfect calendar and clock. Newton was scheduled to sail upriver a couple of days earlier, which would have put him hopelessly out of reach of the coast. But they waited by the coast for those days, hoping to trade for a few last articles from the next ship to pass by to complete their supplies for the journey. It was not even the right time to check for passing ships, but a co-worker went to the shore and saw this ship just beyond the right distance for an easy anchor point. He signalled, and the ship stopped and sent a boat to trade.

One of the first questions asked by the boat was about Newton! So in February of 1747, the ship's captain came to rescue John Newton on behalf of the ship's owner, Captain Newton's friend. Really, this rescue came from God himself! Interestingly, Newton had grown so comfortable that he was deciding that he preferred to stay in Africa. Not to be denied, however, the captain completely made up a story about an annual allotment from a distant relative's passing away waiting for John in England. Newton was not ultimately moved by the money, but then he remembered the girl. The thought that he could see Polly again recaptured his motivation. And now with his new money, perhaps he would even have grounds to pursue marrying her. This was enough to get John off the island and onto the boat. Fifteen months of captivity finally ended!

3

I WAS BLIND, BUT NOW I SEE

This slow rescue mission still had a long way to go to find completion. Remember, this was Captain Newton calling in a favour from a friend back in Liverpool, who had put his captain on the lookout for John. Although the business of the voyage had been proceeding for four months, it would require more than a year's time still to complete. The *Greyhound* was no slave ship. These men were trading for gold, ivory, types of wood, and beeswax. These sorts of items took longer to collect and would send the sailors searching much further south than Newton had previously travelled. Keep the contents of their cargo in mind for later in the story. Even the very materials on Newton's rescue ship were stamped by God's hand, as we will soon see!

Another way the *Greyhound*'s captain persuaded Newton to join his ship was the promise of sleeping in his own cabin, eating at his table, and having no responsibilities onboard. While this must have offered a welcome respite for him in contrast to his many months of African servitude, God did not make men to be idle. The ungodliness of Newton's heart which had been pounded into dormancy as far as manifesting itself on the Plantanes was concerned began to awaken. He compared his former situation to a dormant tiger with nothing to eat and nothing to do. The wild animal was not tame; it simply had no opportunity to express itself! This sinful tiger, John Newton, now with a full belly, no responsibilities, and nothing to do but a little mathematics, started expressing itself once again.

The boundaries of the blasphemies of John Newton were energetically tested and pushed further. The creative heart God gave him was used to make up fresh profanities every day. Although not religious, the captain often seriously rebuked his foul-mouthed passenger. He even reached for a biblical character reference and called John a Jonah on his ship whenever anything bad happened on the voyage! I wonder whether the captain had read just how badly things went on Jonah's ship before he started throwing that label around!

As at other times in his life, it seems as though God directly intervened to keep Newton alive long enough to repent of his sins. For all of his flaws, John was not a regular indulger in serious alcohol. But he was so driven to entice others into sin and trouble that one time he arranged a drinking competition. When he and the others were quite drunk, John's hat flew overboard while he danced about like a maniac. His untrustworthy eyes saw the ship's boat over the rail and he eagerly lunged towards it to catch his hat. The boat, however, was too far away to help him. In another second, stuporous non-swimming Newton would have plunged

into a watery grave; but someone equally drunk grabbed his
clothes and tugged him back onto the deck. Another time,
he and a few others went hunting off the ship. They were
successful and brought half of their spoils back to the boat.
Although they had marked the location of the rest of their
meat, they became terribly lost in swampy woods infested
with deadly animals. Even the light of the moon and the
stars eluded the hopeless party. After they had spent hours
aimlessly wandering, the moon finally appeared through
the thick clouds. It revealed that they had been wandering
even deeper into the interior. Eventually God allowed them
to make it back to the coast, although far afield from their
entry point. These divine deliverances made no impression
on Newton, as his conscience seemed dead.

When they had finished their business, it was, at last, time
to return to England. They were so far south, however, that
currents and trade winds forced their path first westward to
Brazil and then north near Canada before they could cross
back to their homeland. They enjoyed fishing for cod off
the coast of Newfoundland. Little did they know that these
fish would soon replace the ample provisions that they were
counting on to sustain them until they returned home.

The beginning of mercy

On 9 March, John Newton had an unusual reaction to
reading *The Imitation of Christ* by the medieval monk,
Thomas à Kempis. As it was one of the few books on board,
he had read it before almost like a novel. This time, however,
a crushing thought crossed his mind: 'What if these things

should be true?' Slamming the book shut, he tried to chase the forceful implications out of his brain.

That very night their ship was attacked by a massive storm. From then on, Newton marked 10 March as the day God began to blast through his granite heart. The tired ship was ill-prepared for the intensity and the duration of this powerful storm. The wood, the mast, the sails, and the cords were already in need of repair. This storm would stretch them to their limits. Newton was awakened to the fury by a desperate cry from the deck. As he ascended the ladder to help, the captain sent him to fetch a knife. The man who replaced Newton on the ladder found the deck and the ocean at the same instant as a massive wave washed him overboard, never to be seen again. God had again saved John Newton. Mourning had to wait as the storm shredded the ship in its very first moments. Imagine nailing your clothes inside boards to form emergency patches for holes in the battered boat! Everyone fought the rising sea-water with the pumps, but the battle was being lost. The crew of eleven or twelve laboured hard to endure, continually pumping and bailing. In God's mercy, the cargo they carried was unusually light. Normally-weighted cargo would have meant disaster, but because beeswax and wood are actually lighter than water, the ship stayed afloat.

After many hours of pumping and trying to keep the disheartened crew motivated, John thoughtlessly made mention of the Lord's mercy in a statement to the captain. Instantly, the significance of his words impressed him. 'What mercy can there be for a wretch like me?' he thought. For almost twenty-four relentless, terrifying hours the storm tossed Newton up and down, either on the pumps or literally tied down on the deck at the helm steering the ship with barely any expectation of survival. His body shaking with chills because of the intense cold, John's soul also shook with reflections of what he deserved from God. He concluded that he was condemned because of his utter disregard for the gospel he once knew. In spite of that, he tried to pray. Not a prayer of faith, or even true repentance, but a creature crying to its Creator.

Finally, the storm abated. They made progress toward their port, but the ship's sails were in tatters, and the currents and weather conditions alternately worked for and against them. Their other supplies had mostly been beaten and destroyed. It would take four more weeks for the battered boat to make it home. They subsisted mostly on the cod they had caught off the Canadian coast. During these days of continued uncertainty Newton used his free time to devour the Scriptures — reading and rereading them, and thinking about what they meant. He prayed for the Lord's mercy and instruction. They finally landed at Lough Swilly in Ireland. Just two hours later, yet another violent wind lashed out so furiously that it would certainly have sunk the sorry ship. God had saved John Newton from the sea, and was beginning to save his soul.

The beginning of hope

After such mercy was shown to Newton and the others at sea, you might assume that John Newton became a Christian. After all, he did cry out to God for mercy, and after the storm he prayed and became a serious student of the Bible. That is all true, but John Newton was not yet a Christian. However, this was the beginning of God's gracious work in his heart.

As the ship was being repaired, Newton's body and soul were also being repaired at nearby Londonderry. He went to church twice a day. He earnestly prayed and sought the Lord. The Bible was Newton's food. He longed for a sense of God's mercy. As he thought seriously about the Scriptures, Newton went from trying to find a foundation to believe them, to assuming they were true for the sake of argument, to believing that they were right, and then searching for evidence that they could offer hope for him in spite of the depths and duration of his sin. He made serious vows to God that he would serve him for ever. Was he a Christian yet? Still no!

You could imagine Newton feeling pretty safe in Northern Ireland, having survived the incredible events at sea. But not many days after his health had returned, he had the opportunity to hunt birds with some of the gentlemen of the city. As he climbed a steep bank, his gun went off so close to his face that it singed the corner of his hat. The thought that the safest place on earth we can be is in the will of God is surely correct! We need God's protection and grace every hour of every day, regardless of where we are and what the outward circumstances appear to be!

When letters from Ireland arrived in England there was relief and rejoicing, as the ship searching for Newton had been gone from home for eighteen months and was assumed to be on the ocean's floor. John's father received the happy notice of his son's rescue mere days before he was to depart for Canada. He was heading to Hudson Bay to become governor of Fort York. Captain Newton was unable to bring his son on the trip because of John's delays in Ireland. They had a good correspondence over the next few years, but unfortunately John's hopes of providing a full apology in person for his years of reckless sinfulness were not fulfilled, as the captain died in Canada some two years later in 1750, without ever returning to England. Before leaving, though, the captain did call on the Catlett family in Kent to offer his full blessing on the prospective marriage of John and Polly.

Upon arrival in England, John eagerly made his way to Kent to see Polly and her family. His dramatic proposal was not really dramatic or even a proposal. He tried to mumble something about his hopes and intentions, but basically he only got out a request to write to her and the question as to whether anyone else was in the picture. She mercifully gave him some hope — yes, she would read his letters, and no, she did not have anyone else after her. He grabbed on to that hope and then he took a long walk. He walked 250 miles back to Liverpool. He needed money and Liverpool was where his contacts for ship jobs were.

Back to the boats

Joseph Manesty was the name of Captain Newton's friend in Liverpool who had sent his captain to look for John on the west coast of Africa. When John finally arrived in Liverpool he was very grateful to Manesty as God's instrument of rescue. Manesty, in turn, continued to show kindness for the son of his friend by offering him the command of one of his ships. Newton declined for the time, preferring first to learn obedience and more of the business as the first mate to the former mate of the ship that rescued him.

Was Newton at last a Christian? Well, it appeared that John Newton was on a path of maturity and Christian wisdom, but he was not yet a believer. His confidence was not entirely in the Lord at this point — he had plenty of self-confidence mingled in his heart. During the voyage, as his officer skills increased, his walk with God became neglected and weak. The devil happily succeeded in dragging Newton back to the swine's slop of sinfulness. While he was not profane, as he had been before, John lost his heart to pray and seek the Lord. He returned to many of his old sinful ways. Even when the ship stopped at the Plantanes, and he saw the very places and people his sinfulness had used to wreck his life, he spiritually sleep-walked through the experience. He noticed the lemon and lime trees that he had planted beginning to grow and close to bearing fruit. Remember those mocking comments of Clow and PI that perhaps by the time those very trees bore fruit Newton would return as the captain of his own ship? Newton did not seem to be impacted by such a remembrance either! He was spiritually shrinking. How could such sights not awaken his heart with gratitude to the God who had delivered him from such a place? We often underestimate the blinding effects of sin. This is the only explanation there can be.

Finally, a violent fever broke open John's chains of sin. The sickness worked like jump leads from a good car shocking the weak battery of another car back to life. His conscience reignited; his desires to pray and pursue Christ awakened at last. He made no more self-confident vows to the Lord. Instead, he leaned as never before on Jesus, who had died and risen again on behalf of sinners like himself. This horrible illness left Newton almost as suddenly as it had put him on his back. Once again, it seemed as if God had custom-designed this trial to get Newton's attention spiritually.

Was John Newton now a Christian? It is impossible to say with certainty, but God was drawing him closer to Christ than ever before. Surely, God was using this painfully slow process to sink into Newton's heart deep layers of appreciation for God's grace that would form the foundation for the rest of his life.

During the eight months of this journey Newton worked to teach himself Latin. The man with only two years formal education (which ended at age ten) used difficult Latin texts and a Latin Bible to figure it out himself. He found himself energized by classical learning.

There were numerous dangers, toils and snares that occurred during this journey. God snatched him out of the jaws of death several more times, once by a seemingly random request of the captain to pull him from his regular boat trip up the river with others to acquire supplies for the ship. That particular boat sank and the man who replaced Newton drowned. Even the pagan captain could not help but see God's hand in preserving Newton's life!

As the ship sailed westward to Antigua and on to Charleston, South Carolina, John had sweet times of fellowship with the Lord. He loved to worship in the cathedral of God's creation, taking long walks in the woods and through fields. He lacked spiritual discernment, though, and his progress was filled with contradictions. He seemed to fail to benefit from hearing good sermons from faithful ministers like Josiah Smith. While he did not join in the worldly amusements of the rougher crowds, he did find himself frequently being with them after hours.

Newton gets the girl!

Seven years had passed since John Newton had first met Polly Catlett. Now, at last, the way was clear for them to be married. Their happy union began on 1 February 1750. Throughout his life Newton expressed concern that he loved this woman so much that it slipped into the realm of idolatry. While that might sound like the passion of a hopeless romantic, his new marriage to his dream girl did turn his heart from the Lord who gave her to him. It was not until he was summoned to Liverpool for a voyage that spiritual things were again brought into sharp focus. The pain of separation drew John to lean on the one who never leaves or forsakes his children.

In August 1750, Newton put on the captain's hat for the first time. He was in command of the *Duke of Argyle*, with a crew of about thirty. He tried to lead them with integrity and even officiated at chapel services twice on Sundays using the liturgy of the Church of England.

Hand-written letters were the communication of the day. It could be six months or more between opportunities to pass packets of mail toward home or the ships abroad. In spite of that time lag, Newton wrote to Polly two or three times a week during his voyages. He would then send the letters all at once. God used all this practice to sharpen his writing skills. One of his most significant ministries in his later years as a minister was his letters to others. These letters not only blessed those that received them, but also others who would read them over their shoulders.

Newton used his time on the ship well. He continued to master Latin, this time bringing a dictionary with him on the trip! His amazing talents for languages, however, would eventually be governed more by his growing love for the Scriptures than his love for classical learning. After fourteen months at sea, God brought Newton safely home on 2 November 1751.

John Newton used the time between his voyages to continue to push forward spiritually. He began to write a diary to help track his spiritual progress. He devoured solid Christian books like Henry Scougal's *Life of God in the Soul of Man*, James Hervey's *Meditations Among the Tombs*, and Philip Doddridge's *Life of Colonel Gardner*. The last of these was a great conversion story of a dragoon commander forsaken by many of his men in battle. It brought John to tears. In spite of his progress, surprisingly, Newton still lacked help from Christian preaching and Christian friends.

His second voyage as captain began the following summer in July 1752, on board a ship called the *African*. This trip included delightful times of solitude for spiritual meditation and communion with God.

God protected Newton carefully on this trip as well. One time, a group of his crew decided to rebel and to turn to piracy. When two of the main ringleaders became ill on the same day, with one even dying, their plot was uncovered and destroyed. Another time, Newton left the *African* to go to shore; but bouncing on extreme surf for more than half an hour prevented him from landing. By not landing, Newton avoided a scandalous accusation plotted against him to wreck his reputation in Africa and even back in England. God took the secret evil plans against his servant and brought them to nothing.

When Newton was not fighting off pirate schemes and false accusations, he disciplined his days by breaking them into three eight-hour slices. He studied for one slice, he spent another on meals and sleep, and the third was devoted to exercise and devotion.

God allowed a great trial to fall on Newton during that voyage. The letters from Polly which he longed to devour were not waiting for him at St Christopher's. They had been forwarded to Antigua by mistake. The only explanation Newton could come up with was that his new wife was dead. As he tried to rest his heart in a sovereign and wise God, he found himself sick with worry and despair. He lost his appetite. He could not sleep. He had a sick pain in his stomach. He was contending with God. The torments lasted a couple of weeks until he sent a small boat over to Antigua. When the boat returned with several packets for him, from his very alive wife, his health returned, along with a healthy dose of humility and shame for his lack of faith and gratitude to his Maker!

There were only six short weeks at home between Newton's second and third voyages as a ship's captain. Again, his charge was the *African*. One of the most striking features of this trip was the presence of Job Lewis, who had been one of his good friends on the *Harwich*. John had made a strong impression on Lewis back in those days; but sadly, the wrong kind of impression. John had intentionally tried to propagate his wild lifestyle, and Job Lewis had become a convert! Now, Newton had the unhappy burden of looking at his former life in a mirror whenever Job was around! John intentionally brought Lewis onto the crew of the *African* with the hopes that he could point Lewis toward the Saviour whom Newton had now found. He shared his story with Lewis and tried to answer all of his objections. Lewis, when cornered, was not afraid to pull out the ultimate excuse that he had learned the lifestyle from Newton himself. What a dagger to Newton's conscience! On the ship, Lewis ran wild. In addition to not following Newton's new example, Lewis actively undermined Newton's influence over the rest of the crew. Eventually, Newton bought a small ship and sent Lewis away on it to trade on his ship's behalf. Newton offered parting pleas to Lewis to turn his life towards righteousness. Initially, Job seemed affected by John's final words, but later Newton's old friend threw off all moral restraint. He then became sick in the heat and apparently died in his sin.

Newton also became quite sick during the passage between Africa and St Christopher's. He thought he might die, but he had a quiet composure. The words, 'He is able to save to the uttermost', brought him great relief. He doubted his salvation during his fever but was also encouraged by the words, 'The Lord knoweth them that are his.' By the time the ship reached the Caribbean, Newton had made a full recovery.

Was John Newton a Christian yet? Through his journey of the past six years since the storm, Newton had read and reread the Bible, as well as many other solid Christian books. He still, however, really had had very little teaching and virtually no mature Christian friends. It seems that he understood and even believed the gospel, but there were gaping holes in his Christian understanding. But on this third voyage, far away from home, God was about to acquaint him with a godly man from Wapping, Newton's birthplace!

The Lord does not intend that his people spiritually prosper in isolation from other Christians. We are made to be interdependent, generally in local church families. In many places, Christians also enjoy close friendships with other believers among other churches. Some true Christians, however, find themselves in seasons of isolation — from other people, or from a healthy local church, or even from Christian friends. John Newton began his Christian life in such a season of isolation. He had had no regular church, no regular preaching, and not one mature Christian friend.

Alexander Clunie was a ship's captain and a mature Christian. Although they were fellow English citizens, and even natives of the very same small town, the Lord introduced these two servants of his on the island of St Christopher's in the West Indies, not far from what is now the Dominican Republic.

Have you met someone in whom you detect a kindred heart for the Lord? King David and Jonathan experienced that almost instant bond of Christian friendship. It seems that that was the case with fellow captains Newton and Clunie, because they became fast friends. They enjoyed a month of excellent fellowship on the island together, spending nearly every night together, alternating on board each other's ship. Some of those conversations went into the small hours of the morning — even until nearly the dawning of the next day. Newton's mind was stretched by Clunie's helpful insights, but his heart was also enlarged with a greater love for the Saviour.

Before this friendship, Newton said he had the basic gospel right, but he also had fears and doubts mixed together with his faith. Perhaps he would backslide again, as he had done as first mate, and as he had done in those first months after he had married Polly. Clunie helpfully pointed Newton to Jesus, his power, and his promises. Newton's fears melted away. At last, six years after the storm at sea when he first cried out to the Lord for mercy, John Newton was a solidly established evangelical Christian.

Captain Clunie also challenged John Newton to go public with his faith and prayers. Not only did he demonstrate the benefits of having Christian friends, Clunie also pointed Newton to some great spiritually-minded contacts back in London. Discernment enables Christians to sort out right from wrong. Experienced believers who know God's word well can think through current issues and make careful biblical evaluations. Up to this point in Newton's spiritual journey, almost everything got through his safety net —

good and bad preaching, good and bad books, and some good and bad practices. Clunie greatly helped Newton to think through some current trends in England biblically. Throughout the rest of their days, God strengthened the delightful friendship of these two men. Some of the letters Newton wrote to Clunie in the 1760s were published as *The Christian Correspondent*. Remember Newton's godly mother, Elizabeth, trying to raise her only son in the ways of the Lord in Wapping? As she prayed and prayed for her little boy, God was at work a couple of streets away in the life of Alexander Clunie. Clunie was a member of the Stepney Meeting, where Samuel Brewer was the minister. Brewer was a good friend of Elizabeth's pastor, David Jennings. Now, twenty-two years after her death, her son would be stamped by the influence of this man in answer to her prayers! Isn't God great?

The journey across the Atlantic Ocean was especially smooth, giving Newton many hours to reflect upon his month of encouragement on the island of St Christopher's. He arrived at Liverpool in August 1754.

The plan was for Newton to be home for a short time. Joseph Manesty had a new ship that was ready to be launched in Captain Newton's charge. Although John Newton did not seem to have any Christian convictions against the slave trade at that time, he commented that he was feeling more and more like a jailer, and hoped and prayed for a more humane line of work. No doubt he also longed to have much more time with Polly. God answered these prayers in a most unusual way. Just two days before he was to leave on the voyage, Newton and Polly were together at tea. Newton experienced some kind of seizure, or perhaps a mini-stroke. It lasted about an hour and left him in poor condition afterwards, being in pain and dizzy. In spite of the fact that such seizures had never happened to Newton before (or later in the rest of his life), it was determined by the doctors and the ship's owner, with agreement from Newton, that he should resign the command of the ship. So Newton's tenure as slave ship captain ended quite suddenly. As we have seen so many times before in John's life, God's hand of protection was at work here as well. The new ship sailed with another man serving in Newton's place. That man died on what would prove to be a tragic trip, which also took the life of most of the officers and some of the crew!

Liverpool

The newly-retired captain left Liverpool for London. His seed package of fresh contacts from his new Christian friend Alexander Clunie was about to germinate into several fruitful new friendships. Right away Newton sought out Clunie's pastor, Samuel Brewer of the Independent church commonly referred to as the Stepney Meeting. Brewer was known for his heart-directed biblical messages throughout his fifty years of pastoral work. The Newtons and Brewers would spend much time together in one another's homes over the next years of their lives. Their Christian friendship expanded as Brewer introduced Newton to the famous evangelist George Whitefield.

These were the days of the Methodists. It was just a few years after the Evangelical Awakening. God raised up men

like John and Charles Wesley and George Whitefield from
within the Church of England to call the church and the
country to repentance and to faith in Jesus. Their attention
to methodical Christian discipline in their spiritual growth
and ministries earned them the nickname of 'Methodists'.
When most of the Anglican churches rejected the men and
their message, they preached in fields to the masses. Tens of
thousands were brought to faith in Christ. Tirelessly, John
Wesley rode his horse some 250,000 miles crisscrossing
England over 50 years. He proclaimed the glad message
some 40,000 times. He organized small groups or societies
of true believers for preaching, prayer and godly interaction
from town to town. In addition to his work in London and
throughout England, George Whitefield also added seven
transatlantic trips to preach the gospel mightily up and
down the eastern seaboard of North America.

Just as it affected tens of thousands of others throughout
England and the colonies that would become the United
States, so the preaching of George Whitefield thrilled John
Newton's heart. He felt the need to write to Polly once
explaining that he needed to prolong his time in London
an extra day just to hear Whitefield preach one more time.
He sounds like a modern child begging for just one more
turn on his favourite video game, except that John Newton
wanted one more turn feeding from one of the most gifted
preachers in the history of the church. John Newton now
saw London as a fountain of gospel truth. He wished for a
bigger mouth to be able to drink it all in. In these days he
also benefited from a growing group of spiritual friendships,
participating in several religious societies.

Although he was making rapid progress in his spiritual growth, Newton had two problems. First, for the first time in his adult life, he had no clear job prospects. The ships had all sailed for the season, so he would not be able to join a voyage, even if he wanted to go back in that direction. His second problem hit even closer to home. His wife was very sick. Polly would never be very healthy. This illness, however, defied the doctors' efforts to explain it. For the next eleven months John Newton thought that his beloved Polly, who was suffering great pain along with other symptoms, would die soon. He was greatly tested in his trust in God.

In August 1755, with the help of his faithful friend Joseph Manesty, he secured an excellent position in Liverpool as Surveyor of the Tides. The job description behind that unusual title is basically that of a customs officer. Six oarsmen rowed Newton in a small boat to inspect incoming ships for contraband. Newton's vast experience on ships (and participating in mischief on those ships!) made him an ideal inspector. He had fifty-sixty men under his charge at the post. The business of the job came in waves, so Newton also had plenty of leisure time for study. In taking the job, he knew he would have to leave Polly with her family. Though it made them both heavy-hearted, it seemed like the best thing to do. Thankfully, God began healing Polly almost the moment her husband left her. Within two months she was able to join her husband in Liverpool, restored to good health.

Compared to the spiritual resources Newton had thrived on in London, Liverpool seemed like a wasteland. His job, however, continued to provide excellent amounts of time which Newton used to get a good return for his labours in study. His desire for the Latin classics needed to decrease so that his direct study and meditation on the Word of God could increase. He read the Bible for as much as three hours per day! First, he took up Greek to be able to read the New Testament and the Greek version of the Old Testament in their original language. When he could do that well, he picked up Hebrew to read the Old Testament. His own opinion of his abilities was a modest report of being able to read the historical books fairly easily, but still struggling with the prophetic and other books, and that he often required Hebrew lexicons and other tools! Two years later he studied Syriac because he thought he could benefit from reading parts of the Bible in another ancient language. Marvel again that John had only two years of formal education, which were not even a good experience!

He aggressively sought to grow in other ways as well. He read great Christian books in English, Latin, and even French. The biography of Puritan pastor Joseph Alleine brought him to tears. He longed for more of the zeal and godly character he saw in Alleine. Prayer and meditation were also abundant in John's life during these days.

One of those times of meditation stirred new desires within Newton's heart. As he considered Paul's words, 'They only were hearing it said, "He who used to persecute us is now preaching the faith he once tried to destroy." And they glorified God because of me' (Galatians 1:23-24), Newton started to think that he too would like to proclaim the gospel that he had long fought against.

John Newton had sought out good Bible preaching in
London, and he rapidly sampled sermons from Liverpool
and the surrounding region. When George Whitefield came
to Liverpool just a month after he had relocated there,
Newton quickly reacquainted himself. While in London, so
many loved Whitefield that it was difficult to have a lot of
personal time with the evangelist. In Liverpool, however,
Newton maximized the opportunity to hear him and
spend time benefiting from Whitefield's wide Christian and
ministry experiences. When Whitefield's time in Liverpool
was over, Newton escorted him out of town, having heard
him preach nine times and having had at least five meals
with him either alone or together with others. Some in
Liverpool even began to call the new Surveyor of Tides
'the young Whitefield'. Whitefield's twin emphases of God's
sovereignty over the salvation of sinners and God's passion
to see the lost saved would mark Newton for ever as well.

The theological split between Whitefield and Wesley over
the doctrines of grace would not hinder Newton's hungry
heart from trying to benefit as much as he could from
both mighty preachers of the gospel. Whenever John
Wesley preached near Liverpool, John Newton sought
to be sitting before him in the pew. Newton gave serious
thought to joining the Methodists more formally and even
becoming one of their travelling itinerant ministers. Polly's
family, however, was much more serious about the Church
of England, and John saw the massive opportunities for
ministry serving within the Established Church. Although
Methodists had the gospel and plenty of zeal for growth
and spiritual ministry, they were quite marginalized and
considered rather negatively in general in England and,

of course, within the Church of England (even though the Wesleys and Whitefield never formally left the Anglican Church). Newton was also conscious of his own broken health and the care of his wife. John's physical troubles were due to his years at sea and especially his years enslaved and malnourished on the Plantanes; and Polly's were due to her weak constitution, which had recently been so tested just as Newton was coming to Liverpool. He did not think he was up to the miles of horseback riding through all kinds of weather that the itinerants were expected to endure. Although his friendship with Wesley would be strained later because of theological differences, Newton always appreciated the godly preacher.

Although the church scene in Liverpool was not very encouraging, Newton did benefit from time among two different Baptist churches in the city, but he never joined either one. However, Newton did find colonies of heaven some distance away in Yorkshire. He made many wonderful friends and benefited from many wonderful sermons. In a time when some counted denominational loyalties very highly, and many within the Church of England looked down on all Methodists within and Dissenters without, Newton stood apart as a model of gospel connections. If a man preached the gospel, and loved the Lord, and the Bible, Newton was drawn to him as a Christian friend. He benefited from preachers of all kinds but was cautious about associating with any one group too closely.

John Newton found a kindred heart in the plain-spoken preacher, William Grimshaw of Haworth. In addition to his local ministry, Grimshaw would preach on a pair of

circuits during the week, totalling twenty-five to thirty
sermons per week. His ministry was a wonderful model
for Newton to study. Grimshaw gave him much counsel
and encouragement about John pursuing the ministry as
well. Henry Venn of Huddersfield also proved to be a wise
and godly mentor to Newton in these formative years.
Newton's network extended to the Baptist John Fawcett, the
Independent James Scott, the Presbyterian John Edwards,
and even the Moravian Benjamin Ingham. Proverbs 13:20
says, 'Whoever walks with the wise becomes wise, but
the companion of fools will suffer harm.' Newton drew
from the personal example of his friends and their Bible-
saturated encouragement, comfort, exhortation and counsel
throughout his life, but the impact was most dramatic in
these early years of Newton's spiritual formation.

Waiting for ordination

As John Newton's knowledge and maturity was on the rise,
his heart was longing to proclaim God's glorious Word
to others as well. He began to take advantage of small
opportunities that the Lord began to bring to him to give a
small word of exhortation and even to preach. He also wrote
spiritual pamphlets and tracts that he passed around to the
churches of Liverpool.

Newton's friend John Edwards asked John Newton to preach
for the first time at an evening meeting. After a sweet time
of fellowship over tea, Edwards pointed Newton to a quiet
room for any final preparation needed. Fully assured in his
preparation, Newton declined, and then went to the pulpit

with no notes. After reading the text from the Bible, John began well. A few minutes in, however, his thoughts flew away like feathers in the wind. Ultimately, he turned the sermon back over to Edwards and shamefully slipped into his seat. For a while when he saw anyone talking in public, he assumed they were discussing his preaching flop! The next time he preached, the pendulum swung the other way. He was a statue in the pulpit, his eyes boring holes into his notes, not daring to look up for fear of losing his place. Instead of being on either extreme, John longed to share faithful messages from his heart to the hearts of his hearers.

Elizabeth Newton had dared to hope that her only son would become a minister of the gospel. Although she poured great amounts of biblical truth into her bright child, after she died, most of her lessons leaked from his unredeemed heart during his years of rebellious decline. As a new Christian, however, John overflowed with new appreciation for his mother, and he tried to recover her sweet influence. As he grew spiritually, God kindled a flame of desire to speak out for him. He wanted to let others know that God's grace was truly amazing — if it was great enough to save a wretch like Newton, he needed to let other wretches know all about it. Of course, his friends were encouraging him along as well. Over the years many Christians have had a heart to preach and minister for the Lord, only to have faithful friends or others in their church wisely discourage them. When God sets a man apart for ministry, it tends to be apparent to the spiritually-minded people closest to him. In John's case, his friends pushed him to continue to pursue ministry. He set apart special time to think about it and purposefully seek the

Lord for his direction. He humbly wrote down his thoughts and prayers about seeking the ministry in a journal of some sixty oversized pages!

A vital question for Newton was whether to pursue pastoral ministry within the Church of England or among the Dissenters. As has been noted, Newton's friendships crossed all boundaries for the sake of the gospel, but he had carefully maintained enough distance from formally joining Dissenters in order to leave the door to the Established Church open. As he compared Scripture to Scripture and began to understand the system the Bible teaches more thoroughly, he thought he might have too many significant quibbles with the *Book of Common Prayer* of the Church of England to be able to subscribe for ordination in good conscience. He felt relegated to the Dissenters, until Rev. Henry Crooke came alongside him and helped him to understand more accurately the meaning and intent of the Anglican Articles and the significance of subscribing to them.

With his conscience calmed, John Newton was offered the title of curate (similar to an assistant pastor) by Mr Crooke in December 1758. The Anglican Church was committed to an educated clergy, which generally meant graduating from either Oxford or Cambridge. For a self-taught man like Newton to be ordained, he needed special letters of reference. The Bishop of Chester countersigned his testimonials and directed him to one Thomas Newton (no relation) who was the archbishop's secretary. As John Newton waited for his interview, Thomas Newton returned with news that the Archbishop would not ordain him. Of course, one had to wonder whether John Newton's friendships with the unpopular Methodists, Wesley and Whitefield, and with various Dissenting ministers, cost him his opportunity.

Although disheartened for a time, Newton submitted papers again in April 1759. This time he was rejected without any explanation. The note only advised Newton to hang on to the job that God had providentially given him! By the next year, he was open to taking a position as lay pastor for three months in an Independent chapel in Warwick during a slow time in the Tides office. The ministry seemed to be fruitful, but he ultimately refused their offers to settle there permanently. He would look back at this experience as his first taste of vocational ministry. Polly was a life-long member of the Church of England, and her family strongly pressed John to stay within the Church.

Over the next couple of years, Newton received other offers from small Independent works to come and minister. By 1762, he was so frustrated with the Church of England that he was ready to break with it for good. It seems that even Polly was reluctantly willing to come along.

It was at this time that John wrote his conversion story to his friend Benjamin Fawcett of Kidderminster in a series of letters. When another friend of Newton's, Thomas Haweis, discovered them, he asked John to expand on them for publication. The final result was Newton's autobiography, *An Authentic Narrative*. It tells his story from childhood, through his time on the slave ships, including the massive storm where he cried out for mercy. It also tells of his rejection for ordination. It ends in Liverpool with John Newton still desiring to preach, humbly waiting on the Lord.

One of the readers of Newton's new bestselling book was the Earl of Dartmouth. Lord Dartmouth offered the curacy of the church in the small town of Olney to Thomas Haweis. Haweis suggested that he offer it instead to John Newton. In spite of Newton's former ordination difficulties, Lord Dartmouth personally called upon the Bishop of Lincoln, who subsequently agreed to interview Newton. In 1764, some six years after Newton was convinced that God wanted him in the ministry, John Newton had an hour-long meeting with the Bishop of Lincoln. Their discussion was cordial, but it did not avoid the points of concern John had with the *Book of Common Prayer*. The result was that the Bishop was satisfied with Newton's fitness for ministry and agreed to ordain him, which finally happened on 29 April 1764.

4

PREACHING THE FAITH HE ONCE SOUGHT TO DESTROY

(1764–1779)

Everyone loves a good race. Anticipation fills the air as the competitors line up at the starting line. As the signal is given, they give it their all trying to outlast their competitors and the conditions, exerting maximum effort to stretch for the finish line. Now, add to that picture female runners, all dressed in old-fashioned kitchen aprons and headscarves and carrying pancakes in skillets! The modern town of Olney, some 60 miles north-west of London, holds one of the most unusual races each spring. The annual Pancake Race fills the market square with spectators watching these local ladies sprint along the road from the festivities of the square to the old parish church each year on Shrove Tuesday (Mardi Gras), the last Tuesday before Lent. The tradition celebrates a housewife who in 1445 was behind in preparing the family's last meal before Lent. She raced to church with her last pancakes, trying to get to the service before the church bells finished ringing. The modern version of the race was established in 1948. The winner receives a kiss from the Ringer of the Pancake Bell. After the winner's name is announced in the church building, the congregation sings 'Amazing Grace'!

When John and Polly Newton arrived in Olney in May 1764, they discovered a small, poor town with a rich spiritual heritage, with a population made up mostly of low-paid, blue-collar workers. Puritans, French Huguenot immigrants, and associates of John Bunyan and George Whitefield had all contributed to the kingdom work that had been begun in Olney before Newton arrived. The River Ouse still winds along just beyond the Parish Church of St Peter and St Paul, the same building that still marks the finish line of the Pancake Race! The beautiful vicarage, the house to be used by the minister and his family, also still stands just across the field from the church building, only a few blocks away from the market square, which now combines old buildings and modern shops, inns and restaurants. A few of the other old buildings still stand, such as the Bull Inn, which continues to operate in the same location as it did in Newton's day. Lace-making also continues in Olney, but in Newton's day French immigrants had made it the town's leading industry, although it was in decline as demand in England dwindled.

Lord Dartmouth was a solid evangelical. He sponsored many wonderful endeavours within his sphere of influence. Technically, the vicar or lead minister of the church in Olney in 1764 was still Moses Browne. He was a good man and had done much good for the people of Olney by faithfully preaching and teaching God's Word and leading many of the townspeople to the Lord. His large family, however, was somewhat in disarray. Like Eli in the Bible, he seems to have been better at publicly preaching the Bible than at privately raising his children in the nurture and discipline of the Lord. When his family troubles affected his ministry, he took a position as Chaplain of Morden College, Blackheath, in Kent, all the while maintaining the title and some of the money associated with the position of leading minister in Olney.

John Newton officially came to the church in Olney (and remained for sixteen years) as the curate-in-charge or associate minister, but he was really acting the part of the lead pastor. Because of Browne's good Bible instruction and personal ministry outside of his home, Newton happily entered vocational ministry in a relatively healthy situation.

In addition to the costs of living provided by Lord Dartmouth, during his days in Olney Newton also stewarded an amount of money some three times larger from the wealthy Christian leader and philanthropist John Thornton to help the poor and to be hospitable in his personal ministry. Thornton, among his other projects, also personally printed large quantities of Bibles, prayer books, and other helpful literature to be distributed by Newton and many other evangelical leaders in England.

Newton began preaching heart-felt Bible messages, and the people began to awaken. Not only from Olney, but also from the surrounding towns and villages, people came to hear the former slave-ship captain proclaim God's living words. He was also a local celebrity author as his autobiography about his conversion was published just a few months after he arrived in Olney. It quickly went through multiple printings and sold well even in other countries. Newton noted that the people in Olney were reading it too. He found them sometimes just staring at him! He had to agree with their wonder about himself! In short order, a gallery needed to be built to accommodate the crowds longing to be seated in the church building. Within three years of his arrival, the church attendance grew from 200 to more than 600 people.

Ministry efforts

Within a month of his arrival in Olney, the new pastor began to enlarge his gospel network. Six or seven other gospel men from the surrounding area began to meet monthly for mutual encouragement and the strength gathered by godly interaction and prayer for one another. The value of such meetings for both new and seasoned pastors is beyond calculation. As the Lord did not design the Christian life to be lived alone but in the community of a church family, it seems that like-minded pastors should wisely help each other by forming bands of brothers as they gather regularly in local areas and in larger conferences. Newton pursued these kinds of friendships everywhere God placed him. The wonderful blessings he had received as a new Christian from his friendships with Alexander Clunie and those with whom Clunie put him in contact were now expanding as he met regularly with these other pastors.

As a new pastor, Newton also saw many opportunities for ministry. As the local minister of the Church of England, everyone in the surrounding areas who was not specifically associated with one of the Dissenting churches saw him as their default minister. Newton tried to leverage this opportunity for the gospel by beginning all kinds of ministry initiatives.

He began a children's meeting, first at the Great House, which was a large unused house owned by Lord Dartmouth, located next to the church building. When the numbers grew too large for the Great House, they moved into the church building itself. It is heartening to realize that children's ministries two hundred and fifty years ago can have so much in common with modern efforts — both in their opportunities and their challenges!

Newton gathered some eighty boys and girls on Thursday afternoons. He spoke to them about Jesus in concrete terms on a level they could understand. He taught them catechism questions, even using a set of simple theological questions and answers from a Dissenting minister named John Mason in order to make Dissenting families feel welcome at the meetings. He also taught them hymns and even gave prizes to those who could memorize and repeat the right answers. As the weeks turned to months, the numbers of children attending ballooned to over 230!

One time Newton took advantage of a teachable moment in the hearts of the children and their families. The opportunity resulted from some of the children expressing displeasure that some of Newton's prizes were given out to the children of Dissenters. Even at such an early age denominational party rivalries can appear, no doubt taken up from the religious attitudes expressed at home. Newton taught the children the evils of such attitudes. John Newton had been a rebellious wretch, and yet Jesus graciously saved him. How could anyone saved by such grace not be gracious to all of the other men, women, boys and girls who had been rescued by that same gracious Saviour? Unfortunately, obstacles such as his travel schedule, the building of the balcony, and an outbreak of smallpox disrupted the momentum of these fruitful children's meetings. Newton was also burdened by some of the rude and reckless children, especially among the boys, who seemed more interested in the prizes than the Scriptures. Does that not sound all too familiar?

Newton also called the church to prayer. The prayer gathering that met on Tuesday evenings was particularly focused and earnest. Newton actually kept the location in such a place as to keep the numbers down in order to try to prevent the intensity from becoming diluted. By 1769, however, they felt that they had to move the meeting to the Great House. Another group began praying at 6.00am on Sunday mornings for the minister and for God's blessings on the ordinances. On Sunday evenings, the Newtons hosted a tea between 6.00pm and 7.00pm for singing and times of prayer. One night they calculated that they had seventy people in their home!

During special times, special prayer meetings developed. In the summer of 1776, the American colonies declared independence from England. The church in Olney met at 5.00am on Tuesday mornings to pray for peace and for their government. These meetings began with as many as 200 praying people.

Some of Newton's ministry initiatives involved doing less. They actually shut down the church occasionally to encourage the people to attend other (Independent) churches that were holding special meetings. If you are more affected by the gospel than by a commitment to your church party, this makes complete sense. For others, however, this practice seemed very questionable. But the Lord's grace prevailed and deep respect and appreciation developed between the gospel men and women of the region. When the Baptist Association meetings were held in Olney, Anglican John Newton participated. In August 1776, he attended the ordination of John Sutcliff, who became the new pastor of the Baptist church in Olney. That year the Baptist Association meeting was held there. The main sessions were held outside in the orchard between John Newton's and William Cowper's homes, with several hundred in attendance, including influential Baptist leaders Andrew Fuller, John Ryland Sr and John Ryland Jr. Several even stayed in Olney after the meetings to hear John Newton preach, and some had stayed with the Newtons in the vicarage throughout the meetings. Many of these men led the way for other British Baptists to come out of hyper-Calvinism, which practically opposes evangelism and missions. These churches and leaders began to embrace a dynamic combination of belief in God's sovereignty in salvation and also in man's responsibility both to preach the gospel and also to believe it. These were the very men who would form the Particular Baptist Society for the Propagation of the Gospel among the Heathen in 1792 and who would launch William Carey (who was briefly even a member of Sutcliff's church in Olney) to India for a lifetime of gospel impact. Many trace the line of this wonderful biblical gospel perspective to these leading Baptist pastors' friendships with John Newton some fifteen years before Carey's ship sailed for India. Imagine what might have happened if Newton, like so many Anglicans of his day (and churchmen of our day!), had tightly restricted his relationships to only those in his own denomination. Newton's acute awareness of God's grace fuelled his extension of graciousness toward others. The King of grace used Newton's gracious extensions to extend his kingdom further!

Family addition

John and Polly had no children of their own, but they adopted two of their orphaned nieces as their own: one girl while in Olney and the second after they moved to London. Newton was so affectionate that you can imagine the jolly pastor being an ambitious and eager dad. But you could also imagine that the fifty-year-old man might be getting more than he bargained for! That may have been the case, but it seems that God gave John grace to love his adopted girls as much as if they had been his from birth. It seems that they also returned that same love and affection for their new parents.

Polly's youngest brother George died in 1774. He was the last surviving parent of five-year-old Elizabeth Catlett, who was called Betsy. No doubt she brought new energy and affection to the vicarage. In 1776, the Newtons took their new daughter to a boarding-school in Northampton, in part because Polly was very ill and her sick father had also come to the vicarage to receive care for the last six months of his life. John also earnestly desired Betsy to receive a wonderful education with the godly oversight of the wife of a Baptist deacon who ran the school. John frequently preached to the students when he visited Northampton. When the Newtons moved to London, Betsy attended Highgate School.

Stories of grace

Two other wonderful stories of Newton's grace-motivated relationships stand out during his years in Olney. John Newton's special involvement in the life of William Cowper and his special impact on Thomas Scott are sweet pictures of amazing graciousness flowing from a man who had received amazing grace!

William Cowper

John and Polly Newton welcomed William Cowper (1731–1800) into their home in Olney for five months in September 1767. He was moving to Olney to be under the faithful gospel ministry of John Newton. Cowper was a brilliant poet — filled with deep emotion and a vivid imagination. He was a dynamic Christian, but he had suffered much throughout his life and was prone to depression. The lives and ministries of Newton and Cowper would become intertwined for the next twelve years at Olney.

John met William in Huntingdon, where Cowper had moved in the summer of 1765. Shy, emotional Cowper had suffered much in his thirty-four years before meeting Newton. After three suicide attempts, God had used Dr Cotton's spiritual and medical counsels at the asylum to save his soul. Cowper had moved to Huntingdon to escape the hustle and bustle of living in London. While there, he formed a friendship with a Cambridge student, William Unwin. Eventually, Cowper moved in with William's parents, the local parish minister Morely and his wife Mary Unwin, and became like an adopted son in the family. For two years William enjoyed Morely's daily interactions over the Bible. A mutual friend suggested that John Newton visit the family because the Unwins were such devout believers. Just a few days before the visit, William's father was thrown from his horse. The accident cracked his skull and proved fatal. Newton arrived at a family in turmoil, and his heart was warm with pastoral compassion. The family strongly felt the need to be fed from God's Word and under the care of a godly shepherd. Newton offered to help them move to Olney, which they did in September 1767.

After five months with the Newtons, William Cowper, Mrs Unwin, Mary's son, and their household servants moved to Orchard Side, right on the market square of Olney. Being located on the square could be hectic, though. Some years later, Cowper would have a mental relapse. After that time, during a town festival when the market square was very noisy, Cowper sought refuge back at Newton's quieter home. That overnight stay ended up lasting for fourteen months.

Orchard Side had a luscious garden, which was linked to the back of Newton's vicarage by a footpath through an orchard. They paid their in-between neighbour a guinea per year for access to this shortcut, which they named the 'Guinea Field'.

Cowper filled his garden with an array of plants and flowers and had many animals, such as large hares, frolicking around. At the back of the garden, there was a small garden-house with a pair of benches on the walls that they called the Summer House. The construction materials of this mini-house offered a respite from the heat to sit and chat, talk theology, and compose hymns.

In a town of blue-collar workers, the Lord provided Cowper and Mary Unwin as substantial Christian friends for the Newtons, with whom they enjoyed a rich fellowship. Cowper and Newton shared insights from the Scriptures, reviewed their latest finished books, took long walks by the river, worked hard on hymns and poems, and generally sharpened one another in every way. In later years, an intellectual neighbouring pastor friend of both Newton and Cowper, William Bull, sometimes joined the conversation, to everyone's delight. The only exception to the joy was that both Newton and Bull sometimes enjoyed smoking their pipes and choked poor Cowper out of the tiny room!

Character and ministry of Cowper

William Cowper focused his mind on God. He studied God's Word and he ministered for God through the church. At Cowper's funeral, Newton said of his friend that no one he knew was as good at interacting with a portion of Scripture or Christian experience.

If John Newton was the curate-in-charge, William Cowper became the curate's curate! He regularly joined John in visiting and ministering to others. At other times he went alone to care for the sick and others in need. He also actively took part in the various prayer meetings.

For a while these two soldiers in the Lord's service had to do their spiritual work separately, as Cowper went to be with his dying brother, John, in 1770. Although they were separated in body, Cowper and Newton's hearts were still knitted together. William's brother was a very liberal minister who did not know the Lord. William searched for ways to point his brother to Christ. John led the church to lift William and his brother up to the Lord continually. Letters flew back and forth, offering updates, encouragements and advice. Before Cowper's brother died, God opened his heart and he understood the truth about Jesus and believed. Cowper rejoiced to tell Newton, who shared the joyful answer to their prayers with the church family.

Cowper had a special place in his heart to reach out to the lace-makers of Olney, some of whom lived next door to him. As the lace-makers worked, they chanted little songs to keep them up to speed. John Newton recognized the potential of putting biblical truth to song. If they could memorize their chants so well, why not give them something eternally better to sing about? John's mother Elizabeth had taught John the brand-new hymns of their near-townsman, Isaac Watts. John's natural gifts of words, rhymes and poetic imagination, which were once used to compose sarcastic, insulting songs about his ship and her captain, would now be used to compose hymns and songs for the people of Olney. John regularly spent several hours of his study time during the week composing a new hymn to go with the message he would be preaching to the people. Who better to join him in hymn-writing than the brilliant poet William Cowper? Together they worked on composing and compiling literally hundreds of hymns, which would eventually be published as the *Olney Hymns*. Before it was completed, however, Newton's co-labourer would have another serious mental collapse.

Relapse

On the first day of 1773, William Cowper felt the ominous dark clouds beginning to descend on his mind again. He had been up and down over the nine years of peace since his time in the asylum, but this was different — far worse. He went to church, enjoyed tea with Newton, and wrote his last hymn, 'God Moves in a Mysterious Way'. The very next day Cowper was so depressed that he was nearly suicidal, wildly hallucinating that God wanted him to sacrifice himself as Abraham was called to do to Isaac. John was called over in the emergency. Although Cowper made progress beyond the edge of suicide, he never really recovered. Cowper never made it back to church, although the steeple was visible from his house. Newton walked with him through this dark valley for the final six years of the pastor's days at Olney. Although Newton confessed that he did not understand all that was going on inside Cowper, he was committed to him in the bonds of gospel love. Their mutual friend William Bull, the Independent minister of the church in nearby Newport Pagnell, proved to be a wonderful friend for Cowper after the Newtons left for London. Bull was well educated, of a similar temperament to Cowper, and had a similar imaginative flair and a similar love for Jesus. Except for the tobacco, of course, they got along very well.

Cowper felt the Newtons' loss deeply when they left Olney. He would see smoke coming from the attic study of the vicarage and become sad at the realization that his friend was gone. Although apart physically, they loved each other to the end, with many letters passing between them. Polly did not write letters prolifically like her husband, but she sent Cowper regular gifts from London. He was especially fond of fresh fish, and he told her that the fish she sent spoke of her affection for him every bit as well as John's letters!

The last years of William Cowper's life were spent in places outside Olney, but his friendship with the Newtons remained firm. He died on 25 April 1800, and his dear brother John Newton preached at the funeral. John warmly commended his faithful friend, even noting that although Cowper could not receive comfort from God's Word, he could certainly give it out.

Olney Hymns

Olney Hymns was finally published in 1779. The project had been on hold for some time as Newton sought to care for his co-author. The project was so linked to their friendship and collaboration together that Newton lost heart in finishing the work alone, but eventually he did complete the task. The hymn-book contains 348 hymns, with sixty-seven coming from Cowper's pen and the rest from Newton. Different categories divide the one book into three. The first category consists of hymns based on a specific text of Scripture. The second comprises songs that relate to some season or event. The final section contains hymns expressing various aspects of progressing through the Christian life.

Olney Hymns was an instant help to churches all over England and it sold half a million copies over the next few decades. While it was not the first book of its kind, evangelical hymn-singing was a relatively recent practice for the Protestants of England at this time. This hymn-book marked the first appearance of such classic hymns as 'Amazing Grace', 'God Moves in a Mysterious Way', 'There is a Fountain', and 'Glorious Things of Thee are Spoken'. Special consideration will be given to some of Newton's hymns in chapter 6.

Thomas Scott

Within a few miles of Olney lay the parish of Ravenstone and Weston Underwood. The curate of that parish was an arrogant unbeliever called Thomas Scott (1747–1821). The man was nearly a Socinian, a group which claimed to believe the Bible, but interpreted it through the lenses of rationalism and ended up denying the Trinity. Scott actually preached against the orthodox gospel and made fun of those who believed in it. He had heard bad things about the new curate of Olney. The word about John Newton was that he was a fine man with regard to his character and performing the duties of a clergyman, but he was riddled with fanatical Methodism.

In January 1774, there were two people in Thomas Scott's parish who were very near to death. They had not called for

Scott to come and see them, and so he did not go. To his shame, however, he discovered that John Newton did go — several times in fact! Whatever he thought about Newton's theology, he admitted that Newton was a better pastor than he was. He determined to do better as a minister. One of the pair had already died, but Scott did go to see the other dying parishioner (just a few doors down from his own house).

At this point, he began writing to John Newton. Newton sent Scott a copy of his recently published book, *Omicron*, which was a compilation of spiritual letters responding to various inquiries which originally appeared in an evangelical magazine. Scott saw this interaction as an opportunity to correct Newton's evangelical views. He aggressively sought to bait Newton into controversy in his letters. Newton would write back as thoroughly as he could, trying to avoid discussing the doctrines with which he knew Scott disagreed. Once, Scott had occasion to hear Newton preach. He did not understand him at all. He even made fun of his message as politely as he could. After nine or ten exchanges by mail, with Scott always trying to provoke and Newton carefully parrying the jabs, only offering slight gospel hints in retort, Scott dropped the issue for a year and a half. He did not see the conversation going anywhere, and he did not want to be connected with Newton in any way.

Discouragement played a part in Thomas visiting John Newton in April 1777. Thomas was so helped by the gracious words of Newton that he could not help wanting more of a friendship. He began sneaking over to see him. He listened to him preach again, but it still seemed foolish to Scott. He thought Newton was a great man, but so misguided that they would never see eye to eye until heaven.

In the course of their interactions, Thomas made more progress in discovering the truth. He suspected that Newton might be right after all. He realized that he had been so arrogant while hearing other people preach that he had never really listened. He decided to give Newton and a few other gospel men a fair try. Every message he heard affected him; he began to feel poorly about himself. Scott had never preached out of his own experience like these men, because he had no spiritual experience!

Thomas Scott became a true believer in Jesus, developing a voracious appetite for God's Word. He studied it carefully and loved to proclaim it to others. He eventually wrote a commentary on the entire Bible! Soon after John Newton left Olney for London, Scott became the curate-in-charge of the Church of St Peter and St Paul in Olney (with one disastrous man who served shamefully for a few weeks in between!). A few years after that, he followed his mentor to London, taking the Chaplaincy of Lock Hospital Chapel. Newton warmly commended him and his London ministry to William Wilberforce, who benefited greatly from hearing the solid gospel man teaching and preaching from the Word of God.

Transition from Olney to London

There was a great fire in Olney in October 1777. Newton actively ministered to those suffering all kinds of needs. He raised some £200 to help, which was a huge sum in that day. Although his heart had gone out to them, his spiritual love for them was not being returned. The next month his weekly lecture fell on 5 November, Guy Fawkes' Day, a holiday that honoured the discovery of Fawkes' plot to blow up the king and the English Parliament by carrying candles and torches through the streets. The people whom he had so practically helped just a few weeks before and had faithfully ministered to over the previous decade and a half broke into a drunken riot. He literally sent out money to keep the mob from vandalizing the vicarage! He had never thought about leaving Olney, but the fact that such a spirit could come out among the younger people made him wonder whether the end of his time there was approaching. He compared these events to the bad things that God often allows to happen just before he does something great, like Pharaoh's hardness and rebellion just before Israel crossed the Red Sea.

As a respected author and popular preacher, John Newton's influence and notoriety had grown far beyond the borders of the country parish of Olney. When his dear friend and benefactor John Thornton sent him a letter proposing that John move to the City of London to become the new rector of St Mary Woolnoth in 1780, it arrived at a strategic moment. This would be the place John Newton would serve his Saviour for the rest of his life.

5

MINISTRY IN LONDON

(1779–1807)

Certain people in history have had remarkable transformations in their situations. I suppose it is most fun to think about those from low circumstances who move to very high situations, but it has worked both ways. In the Bible, Job certainly was at the top of his field. We do not know too much of his circumstances in comparison to those around him, but we know that he was living well enough for the devil to bring it up to God as the reason for Job's faithful service. If you know the story, you know that God allows the devil to take everything away from Job except for his life (he also kept his wife, but given her counsel to curse God and die, I am not sure whether that was from God or the devil!). After God appeared at the end of the test, Job had his life gloriously restored. Joseph, on the other hand, is an example of simply going from the lowest of the low to the highest of the high. He endured thirteen years of bad days! I am sure that God gave him grace to have joy in difficult circumstances, but it must have seemed as though all his faithfulness was rewarded with even worse circumstances. He went from slavery, to prisoner, to forgotten dream interpreter, until he eventually became Pharaoh's second-in-command in all of Egypt. David was another biblical example. He went from stinky shepherd-boy to God's chosen king of Israel. That journey took him through a few caves and some time in Philistine territory while the current king was trying to kill him, but God put David on the throne in the end.

When John Newton arrived in the City of London to become the rector of the Church of St Mary Woolnoth, he marvelled at his life circumstances. The church was located prominently in the business district of one of the leading cities in the world. Today, the dignified building stands just across the street from the Bank tube station. The Lord Mayor of London lived within Newton's parish! Newton and Polly lived in a very pleasant house on Charles Square, Hoxton, about a mile north of the church and the smoke of the city. God (and only God could do such a thing) had spiritually and physically rescued a miserable rebel sinner who had once been enslaved in the Plantanes off the west coast of Africa and placed him in the centre of the world to tell everyone how great God is!

Sadly, there were not too many other men proclaiming God's glorious grace in London when John and Polly arrived there in December 1779. London had a population of about 950,000, but when Newton arrived, the city — which just forty years before had thronged to hear George Whitefield and John Wesley — now only had one other evangelical Anglican minister serving in a London city church, William Romaine. The bishops and archbishops did their very best to keep Methodistic gospel preachers out of the Established

Church pulpits of the city. This sounds bad, but it was not the whole story of London's spiritual state when Newton arrived. In addition to the Church of England there were Baptists, Methodists (who had virtually separated themselves from the Church of England by this time), Presbyterians, and Independent churches with gospel men labouring hard to minister in accordance with God's Word. And within the Anglican Church, wealthy evangelicals sponsored private chaplains who preached and lectured at a handful of chapels and meeting-places around the city. Still, the spiritual state of the capital was weak; but God in his mercy was changing the circumstances of the city as he had changed the life-situation of his servant John Newton.

The situation and the opportunities in London were quite different from the country town of Olney, but the hearts of the people were the same. You do not have to have money to love money. You do not have to be worthy of godhood to act as proudly as if you are a rival deity. The better-educated and wealthier members of the church and community of London had different temptations from those at Olney, but similar needs. Newton knew this and engaged the people with the same strategies as he had used throughout his ministry — preach God's Word, pray for the people, and spend time with them, applying God's truth personally to their lives.

The notes Newton wished to strike as he took the pulpit of St Mary Woolnoth were those of grace and truth. The gospel-seasoned preacher took Ephesians 4:15 as the basis for his first sermon — speaking the truth in love. He followed that message with sermons from the famous love chapter of the Bible: 1 Corinthians 13.

Ministry opportunities in the church

With the goal of reaching out to the families within the parish who were not regular church attenders, the new pastor had his first message printed to be distributed to every home in the district. He did this at other times as well, seeking to show that, as the new preacher, he was proclaiming a new message in the old pulpit.

The church was soon full of regulars and guests. In fact, some of the members began to complain that the visitors were stealing their regular seats! As they had done at Olney, the people soon built a gallery in the London church to help accommodate the growing numbers. Because of the location within the business district of London, Newton was conscious of the fact that on any given Sunday a prominent banker or businessman could walk into the building. He preached shorter messages and more cautiously on Sunday mornings. He was eager to reach people where they were, giving them the milk they needed to bring them to the place of being able to receive the meat of God's Word. Great diversity marked those who quietly came to hear John preach. His consistent gospel priorities and hatred for party spirit among Christians made hearers from all kinds of religious backgrounds feel most welcome.

John Newton was not above being opportunistic for the gospel. For example, in 1785, London planned numerous celebrations of Handel's Messiah on the occasion of the centenary of Handel's birth. The soloists were prancing about the town like rock stars of the day. Newton captured the wave of excitement by preaching an extended series of messages from the passages in the Bible which Handel used to create his classic oratorio. Newton captured the attention of music fans and directed them beyond the beautiful music of Handel's Messiah to the more beautiful, transcendent Messiah, Jesus Christ. These sermons were then published as a book.

Ministry opportunities in the home

The Newtons had a very open home. Polly has often been compared to an innkeeper. Certainly she saw hospitality as a great opportunity for ministry. Times of family devotion in the mornings and evenings often included non-family-members who had dropped in. Like a father speaking to his children, the seasoned gospel minister used these times of Scripture reading and prayer to make a few pointed comments, often noted for their heart-level applications. Tuesday and Saturday evenings were also open-house evenings for pastors to drop in. Young ministers from all kinds of church backgrounds would regularly join John in the study for a time of conversation filled with instruction, encouragement and counsel. How many churches and even foreign mission fields directly or indirectly benefited from the spiritual delicacies that dropped from the bounty of the Newtons' table and through John's follow-up letters will only be known in heaven.

It is as if John was skipping spiritual stones from the banks of the River Thames in London, stones which then bounced along with gospel impact creating wider and wider ripples. The visitors to the Newtons' home included Christian leaders and missionaries such as Charles Simeon, the Cambridge minister; Simeon's curate and pioneer missionary, Henry Martyn; the poet and playwright turned tract-writer and educational reformer, Hannah More; William Jay, the pastor of a church in Bath for sixty-two years; and the father of modern missions, William Carey, as well as some of his colleagues. The refrain of the reports of these informal meetings was consistent encouragement and spiritual wisdom.

Others in need of spiritual and even material support would find the Newtons' home in Charles Square (and later within the black-brick Coleman Street buildings nearer to the church) one of the best refuges in London. Some days the stream of visitors began at breakfast and finished at bedtime!

Ministry in the city

Within a few years of arriving in London, John was laying the gospel groundwork for a network of gospel men, ministers from various backgrounds, and leading laymen. This group of men met fortnightly for many years. They became known as the Eclectic Society. Edifying banter bounced between biblical, theological and practical topics, and even issues of national importance. As Newton was the senior man, he set the tone for the discussions. The legacy of this gospel group reached beyond the personal benefit they enjoyed from each other. They would also found a significant Christian journal called the *Christian Observer*, and what later became the Church Missionary Society.

John's gospel impact was also felt throughout the city via the messages he gave in the wealthy homes of as many as twenty influential local citizens. His voice within the city was growing ever more powerful for the truth of God's word of grace.

Ministry opportunities in the country

In the summer months, John and Polly generally took a holiday for a month or two based with friends somewhere in the country. These times gave Newton opportunities to strengthen friendships and to usefully fill pulpits far beyond his home region. Even when he visited one of his friends, he tried to have prayer with them and to offer brief expositions of the Bible during morning and evening devotional times. Stories are told of some who came to Christ during these mini-messages.

Ministry opportunities out of the box

William Bull, the Dissenting minister from Newport Pagnell, near Olney, remained very close to Newton throughout his lifetime. Young ministerial prospects among the Dissenters were limited in their training opportunities. The doors of the two English universities, Cambridge and Oxford, were both closed to these men. Bull wanted to establish a training centre, and he sought Newton's help in putting together the curriculum. Although it seemed odd for the training regimen of Dissenting ministers to be established by an Establishment minister (and one without any formal education to speak of!), Newton gladly offered Bull his complete support and assistance. Once again, the effect of God's amazing grace on Newton was to reach outside of his party lines to advance the kingdom of grace by seeking to train more gospel men. The Dissenting Academy, which began meeting in Bull's home, was wonderfully used by the Lord for decades to train men for the ministry in England and for missions to many other countries.

Ministry opportunities in the letter box

John Newton often followed his engaging personal ministry with a stream of useful ministry letters. His letter-writing will be considered in more detail in chapter 7, but it is important not to miss this part of his days in London. He often had stacks fifty high of letters in need of response. His responses were so useful that they were collected and published in magazines and books. Some of Newton's works were written as books, or collected sermons; but many of his most poignant writings, including his autobiography, were written in the form of letters.

John Newton's ladies

John and Polly had adopted their precious niece Betsy in 1774, while they were still living in Olney. A second adopted daughter was added to the Newtons' London home in Charles Square in 1783. The Newtons had enough love to bring another of Polly's nieces into their family. Eliza

Cunningham was the daughter of Polly's sister Elizabeth. Elizabeth's family had one by one died of consumption (tuberculosis). The Newtons sought to comfort the dying mother by assuring her of their love for her daughter. The cousins then became sisters by adoption, and the aging couple became parents once again! The disease that had wrecked her entire family was also attacking Eliza's young lungs. She came into the home as a sick twelve-year-old.

The Newtons expended great efforts trying to care for their new daughter. Doctors' common medical counsel during that period in time involved visiting the sea for fresh air. They spent time on the coast on several different occasions, which were of varying degrees of help to Eliza. Her seasons of recovery turned into a steady decline. As she grew weaker in body, however, she grew stronger in spirit. God gave her tremendous grace to die well, full of faith and of the Holy Spirit. The fourteen-year-old girl became a great encouragement to everyone who spent time with her. John was asked about her energetic testimony of faith so often that he wrote her story, highlighting her character and her death. She died in October 1785 at the age of fourteen years and eight months.

The family's grief over the loss of Eliza was just subsiding when a lump was discovered in Polly's breast three years later. The doctors determined that it was a cancerous tumour too large to operate on. Her condition continued to advance, but even in the spring of 1789 she was able to do some travelling. Her decline was slow and gradual, but God continued to sustain John through the long heartbreaking months of caring for his dear wife. He was still able to eat, sleep, and even preach during her final month. It seems that

God kept one of John's eyes fixed on heaven as he walked through this earthly agony.

Polly Newton died on 15 December 1790. The next week, John preached at her funeral through his tears. He had been intentionally saving the text Habakkuk 3:17-18 for the occasion. It says:

Though the fig tree should not blossom,
    nor fruit be on the vines,
the produce of the olive fail
    and the fields yield no food,
the flock be cut off from the fold
    and there be no herd in the stalls,
yet I will rejoice in the LORD;
    I will take joy in the God of my salvation.

God strengthened Newton's heart to commit his dearest earthly love to the Lord. This was the woman who had sustained Newton for several years before he became a Christian. This was the woman whom he had confessed to nearly idolizing. He compared his situation to David's prayers for his dying son. When the baby died, God helped David to leave the matter in God's wise hands. John was grateful to God for the forty years that he and Polly had enjoyed together as husband and wife. He commemorated the day of her death for the rest of his life with special time alone, reflecting on God's blessing to him and Polly. He even composed sonnets in her memory.

Betsy enjoyed the affection and attention of her father in these years after the loss of Polly. She travelled with John on some of his ministry trips to the country in the summer. However, Betsy was seized by a nervous disorder in 1801. The heavy weight of concern stretched the seventy-five-year-old Newton to his limits. Betsy entered the famed London asylum of Bedlam for twelve long months. The concerned father, with failing eyes, had to be helped as he walked in to see her every day, offering many prayers for her recovery. He waited near her window until he was told that Betsy had waved her handkerchief, the signal acknowledging his arrival. Newton exclaimed that God was calling old Abraham to give up his Isaac. As Isaac was restored to Abraham, Betsy was also restored to her dear father. In just a few years, Betsy married an optician named Joseph Smith, with Newton's shaky hand signing the register on 2 May 1805. The three of them lived together in Newton's home in the Coleman Street buildings. Betsy looked after her adopted father until the end of his life. She walked with him, she read to him, and she even divided his food.

William Wilberforce and the abolition of the slave trade

Of all of the relationships John invested in for the gospel's sake, perhaps his interaction with William Wilberforce resulted in the greatest earthly change for the most people. William was a young man when his father died. His mother sent him to Wimbledon to live with his Aunt Hannah's family. Hannah was a solid evangelical Christian who had regular interactions with the Newtons in both Olney and London. William stayed in the vicarage in Olney and heard Newton preach. He looked up to Newton as a father figure. John saw William as a young man of great potential and began praying for his conversion to Christ. When his mother realized that the evangelical 'Methodists' might be getting to her son, she brought him back home to Hull.

In 1780, William became the Member of Parliament for Hull. While John rejoiced with Hannah about her nephew's new opportunities, William frittered away those years by partying and gambling. He was not concerned about the Lord or about many of his responsibilities as an MP. Five years later the freshly re-elected Wilberforce travelled about Europe with a friend. He spent time reading the Bible and also Philip Doddridge's popular evangelical book, *The Rise and Progress of Religion in the Soul of Man*. Interestingly, the copy of the book he was reading belonged to William Cowper's friend William Unwin, with whose parents Cowper lived. Wilberforce became convinced of biblical truth. He sought to test the promises of God revealed in the Bible and found them to be true. God opened his heart and he became a true believer in Jesus. Zeal consumed the new Christian as he sought to work out the implications of the lordship of Jesus in every area of his life. He began to consider ministry as a vocation instead of politics. He needed help to sort out the conflict in his heart.

William wanted to meet with his old pastor friend from Olney, who now served in London. A problem, in Wilberforce's mind, lay in being spotted in the city as a Member of Parliament with a known Methodist sympathizer such as John Newton. He proposed a secret meeting in December 1785. Wilberforce cautiously approached Charles Square, taking care that he was not being followed. Nervously, he walked around the rectangular square twice before gathering the courage to knock on Newton's door. His nerves quietened quickly as Newton warmly welcomed him in. William was struck as Newton told him of his frequent prayers on his behalf. Newton delightfully listened to his story and his passion to serve the Lord. He then encouraged him to continue to serve the Lord as a Christian in politics, as Joseph and Daniel had done in the Bible. This was a major turning-point in William's life.

Over the next weeks and months Newton continued to mentor Wilberforce with helpful counsel, book recommendations and letters. Wilberforce shook off the secrecy and became a regular visitor to the Newtons' home and St Mary Woolnoth. William also benefited wonderfully from the ministry of John's friend, Thomas Scott, who had moved to London by then. John commended Thomas as a faithful preacher of God's Word, and William gratefully drank in the truth. When William wrote a book, called in recent times *A Practical View of Christianity*, Newton was one of its biggest publicists. He was thrilled at the thought that the Lord might use it in the lives of many in the upper class who would never have been drawn to most other Christian authors.

Newton and Wilberforce's partnership would accomplish much good in England and abroad. They spoke often and enjoyed a steady stream of correspondence. Newton offered counsel, encouragement, and even written prayer-benedictions in his letters to William. Wilberforce influenced the placement of a chaplain on the fleet of the first settlers to Australia. He also helped several evangelical ministers to get through the Church of England's system and to be placed in churches in need of gospel men. But certainly the greatest work of these two men went toward the abolition of the slave trade. Newton began speaking publicly and privately of the horrors of the slave trade. It seems that in his later years, he began to see it as more and more horrible and was increasingly disgusted with his former participation in it. Wilberforce became fully persuaded of the need to outlaw the practice. Sadly, much of the country and many of her leaders were blind to the realities behind the big business.

The former slave ship captain came out from behind the scenes of passionate but quiet encouragement to join the front lines of the battle. John Newton's first-hand experiences were put on paper in January 1788 in his powerful pamphlet entitled *Thoughts Upon the African Slave Trade*. In this brief work, Newton exposed England to what happened in between their perceptions of happy boats leaving with supplies and returning with coveted goods from the New World. He told of the brutal conditions that killed many sailors and the far worse conditions that led to the physical and sexual abuse of so many Africans. He counteracted racial preconceptions about the characters of Africans. The next month, Newton testified before a council of special advisors to the king. In May 1790, he spoke as an expert witness before a subcommittee of Parliament. The battle for the hearts of England and her leaders raged on and on, as greed continued to blind powerful blocs of voters time and again. Newton continued to pray and lift the weary hands of Wilberforce for the fight. Just months before John Newton's death on 25 March 1807 Britain's slave trade was legally abolished as Wilberforce's perennial bill became the law of the land.

John Newton's passage to paradise

The preacher at St Mary Woolnoth was still animated in the pulpit even at age eighty. He was nearly blind and too deaf to participate in conversations. His memory was failing, but his spirit was strong. He loved the truth and still had many wise judgements to offer. It was not long, however, before his friends tried to suggest that he step back from his public ministry. 'What!' he replied: 'Shall the old African blasphemer stop while he can still speak?' His heart tried to keep going longer than his mind was able to be effective. The film *Amazing Grace*, which was mainly about Wilberforce's efforts to abolish the slave trade, rightly quoted the aged John Newton as remarking that while he could no longer remember much, he did remember two things: 'I am a great sinner, but Christ is a great Saviour.'

John Newton died well on 21 December 1807, full of faith. He was buried in a vault under the Church of St Mary Woolnoth near the caskets of his wife Polly and his adopted daughter Eliza. Newton wrote his own simple epigraph:

JOHN NEWTON
ONCE AN INFIDEL AND LIBERTINE
A SERVANT OF SLAVES IN AFRICA
WAS
BY THE RICH MERCY OF OUR LORD AND SAVIOUR
JESUS CHRIST
PRESERVED, RESTORED, PARDONED
AND APPOINTED TO PREACH THE FAITH
HE HAD LONG LABOURED TO DESTROY

In 1893, Newton and Polly's remains were removed during the construction of the London Underground's Bank station. They were reinterred in the church graveyard behind the parish church at Olney, where they remain to this day.

6

THE SONGS OF THE SOUL

The greatest commandment, according to Jesus, is not just to love God with all your mind. No matter how comprehensive a person's understanding of the Bible or how many doctrinal dots they can perfectly connect, if that person does not respond to the truth with warm-hearted affection and faith, they will never be pleasing to the Lord. The greatest commandment is, 'You shall love the Lord your God with all your heart and with all your soul and with all your mind' (Matthew 22:37). God wants the whole of our being — mind, will and affections — to be gripped by love for him.

John Newton had such a heart of love for the Lord, coupled with an acute appreciation for the wondrous gift of mercy that God had given him through Christ's work. These kinds of affections must be expressed. The Bible prescribes singing as one important means of expressing such feelings: 'Is anyone cheerful? Let him sing praise' (James 5:13). Although most of the sacred music of Newton's day consisted of singing psalms and liturgical songs, evangelical hymns or gospel songs were beginning to be used more widely. Isaac Watts had pastored a church just a few minutes' walk from Newton's childhood home in Wapping. Newton's mother had made him memorize some of Watts' new hymns when John was a boy. Since Watts maintained a good friendship with John's boyhood pastor, David Jennings, and even shared his pulpit on occasion, it is likely that John Newton heard the preaching of 'the father of modern hymnody'. As a mature Christian man and minister of the gospel, John Newton loved the model of musical expression that Watts and others had established. With a flaming love for the Lord and a poetically gifted mind, John Newton joined the happy practice of applying his heart to composing hymns for his congregation.

God created music as a part of this beautiful world. He then gave his creatures the opportunity to take up music and to express their intelligence and artistry, declaring the worth of their Creator. The Bible tells us that God expects his people to sing to him, and he implies that he likes it when we do it well and with our hearts engaged. 'Oh sing to the LORD a new song, for he has done marvellous things! ... Make a joyful noise to the LORD, all the earth; break forth into joyous song and sing praises! Sing praises to the LORD with the lyre, with the lyre and the sound of melody! With trumpets and the sound of the horn make a joyful noise before the King, the LORD!' (Psalm 98:1, 4-6). The songs God's people sing on earth are like choir practice for our singing around God's throne in heaven! 'And they sang a new song, saying, "Worthy are you to take the scroll and to open its seals, for you were slain, and by your blood you ransomed people for

God from every tribe and language and people and nation, and you have made them a kingdom and priests to our God, and they shall reign on the earth'" (Revelation 5:9, 10).

A hymn is more than a statement of truth. It stretches the tools of language to express the truth with appropriate passion. Instead of simply offering the facts about God, a text of Scripture, or Christian experience, hymns express those realities through rhythmic language, often using rhyme, symbols and graphic imagery to help the singers feel the facts. When musical melodies accompany these verbal expressions, the emotional elements intensify.

Hymns have the power both to *express* passionate praise and thanksgiving, and also to *inspire* it in others. People often assume music in worship to be one-dimensional — individual believers singing to the Lord. But the Bible depicts God's people singing God's praises together as church families. The Bible also includes a horizontal dimension of Christian song-singing. Paul says believers are to 'Let the word of Christ dwell in you richly, teaching and admonishing one another in all wisdom, singing psalms and hymns and spiritual songs, with thankfulness in your hearts to God' (Colossians 3:16). Hymns sung from the heart encourage, comfort, admonish and inspire the singers at the same time as the Lord is being praised.

John Newton already loved singing hymns before he arrived at Olney. He talked about singing joyful songs to the Lord while walking in fields alone and also along with others in society meetings in Liverpool. Records show that he often enjoyed the accompaniment of instruments like the

German flute and the harpsichord. He even wrote several
hymns while he lived in Liverpool. But Olney is the town
most associated with Newton and his hymns. His desire to
serve that needy place drew out scores of songs from his
heart. Because of their special usefulness at the church in
Olney, especially at prayer meetings, and no doubt because
of the presence of his partner-in-poetry, William Cowper,
almost every hymn John Newton is famous for was penned
in that town. The manual labourers of Olney, particularly
the lace-makers, spurred this along as they would sing and
chant while they toiled at their work. Newton used this
unexpected opportunity to fill the hearts of the town with
God's truth by writing new songs to correspond to the
things he preached about. In the preface to his *Olney Hymns*
(first published in 1779), Newton revealed his intentions.
His design flowed from 'a desire of promoting the faith
and comfort of sincere Christians' and his wish to create a
'monument, to perpetuate the remembrance of an intimate
and endeared friendship' with William Cowper (*The Works
of John Newton*, reprinted by The Banner of Truth Trust,
Edinburgh, 1988, 3:301).

The lyrics of these hymns brimmed with biblical truths,
theological thoughts, and expressions of their spiritual
experience. The imagery impressed the truths upon even
the simplest of his townsmen's minds. The rhymes and
rhythms reminded everyone of the words. Musical tunes
tied the truth to the hearts of the people of Olney and the
surrounding towns and villages. Some weeks Newton spent
as much time composing a new hymn as he did preparing
the new sermon!

Many of the 348 hymns in the *Olney Hymns* were bound to the time and circumstances of their composition, although the spiritual content frequently has had a broader usefulness. A handful of the hymns first published in 1779, though, have truly resonated in the hearts of God's people all over the world for over two hundred years! A selection of John Newton's hymns can be found in most hymn-books, and some of his other lyrics are re-emerging joined to fresh tunes to serve a new generation. John Newton's passion for Jesus Christ, his gratitude for the gospel, and his pastoral desire to inspire such passion in the hearts of the people of God flow out through his hymns. Let us consider a few of his best-known works.

'Amazing grace'

John Newton's best-known hymn had an unusual original title: 'Faith's Review and Expectation'. That title alluded to John's twenty-year practice of starting each new year by looking back at his life and thinking about the future. He took advantage of the change of calendar to give himself a thorough spiritual inspection, reflecting on God's many mercies to him personally. He committed himself to live each new year in the light of God's grace. The intense appreciation for God's favour expressed in this hymn has echoed from the heart of Newton into the hearts of God's people across the boundaries of time, culture and space.

When connections are made between the text listed in the hymn-book and Newton's diary entry, it seems that this song was composed for the meetings of New Year's Day 1773. Newton had used a book of 300 oversized pages as a diary for the previous sixteen years. This particular new year his reflections stretched back a long way as he closed the book on that diary and began a new one in 1773. The sermon Newton preached on 1 January 1773 was based on David's prayer in response to God's amazing covenant with Israel's king that through his offspring there would come the king who would reign for ever. David responded with great humility. His prayer begins with David utterly amazed at God's grace to him:

> Then King David went in and sat before the LORD and said, 'Who am I, O LORD God, and what is my house, that you have brought me thus far? And this was a small thing in your eyes, O God. You have also spoken of your servant's house for a great while to come, and have shown me future generations, O LORD God!'
>
> (1 Chronicles 17:16-17).

Newton had no trouble making the connection: David's promise was fulfilled in Jesus, who in turn has blessed believers with heavenly treasures by God's grace. We too can reflect upon God's incredible dealings with us.

The first day of January 1773, the pastor of the parish church in Olney encouraged his hearers to join him in looking back at their lives and pondering God's undeserved goodness to them. They could be confident that the same great grace which had saved them would sustain them for ever. He then taught the people a brand new song to reinforce this wonderful reminder to be amazed by God's grace. The tune so closely connected to this hymn would not have been used by the English congregation on that first Sunday. The tune called *New Britain* (now often known as *Amazing Grace*) was not married to the words of the hymn until 1835 in William Walker's *Southern Harmony*. The celebration of the past and future grace of God, however, has been sung joyfully to different tunes ever since that January in Olney.

> Amazing grace! (how sweet the sound!)
> That saved a wretch like me!
> I once was lost, but now am found,
> Was blind, but now I see.
>
> 'Twas grace that taught my heart to fear,
> And grace my fears relieved;
> How precious did that grace appear,
> The hour I first believed!
>
> Through many dangers, toils, and snares,
> I have already come;
> 'Tis grace has brought me safe thus far,
> And grace will lead me home.
>
> The Lord has promised good to me,
> His word my hope secures;
> He will my shield and portion be,
> As long as life endures.
>
> Yes, when this flesh and heart shall fail,
> And mortal life shall cease:
> I shall possess, within the veil,
> A life of joy and peace.

The earth shall soon dissolve like snow,
The sun forbear to shine;
But God, who called me here below,
Will be for ever mine.

John Newton did not restrict his thoughts to a clinical analysis of the raw facts of God's mercy. His emotions snatched his true thoughts and exploded them into amazement! The one who had rebelled against the teachings of his godly mother, who had ignored the countless numbers of occasions on which God's hand had kept him alive, who had sought to turn blasphemy into an art form, and who had rebelled to such a degree that he thought he was beyond salvation, was fully amazed at God's grace.

Any Christian should join in the harmony of the chord Newton struck. The degree of a person's amazement about God's grace directly corresponds to their apprehension of the absolute holiness of God and the filthy depths of our rebellion against his will and his ways. Of course, the more pure the Creator is in one's mind the more disgusting the sins of his creatures become. To span the gulf between a holy God and sinful man requires an enormous bridge. When modern evangelists try to illustrate that gulf, they sometimes picture the cross of Christ as a little bridge over what looks like a small stream. When God is not seen as holy and his creatures more or less just need a spiritual tune-up, the degree of amazement over God's grace diminishes. John Newton had a clear vision of his former life. He had no trouble indicting himself as a blind wretch, who was lost in his sinfulness. He also recognized the magnitude of God's mercy toward him as God saved him, found him, and gave him his spiritual sight. The very sound of such grace was sweet to Newton. His did not think of God's grace merely as beneficial, like appreciating the value of green vegetables. He delighted in God's sweet grace as if tasting a delicious dessert.

In the second stanza, we see that a right view of what God accomplished on the cross can have a dual effect with regard to personal fear. On the one hand, the first glance at grace includes a realization of the depth of guilt and responsibility for one's sin. On the other hand, this same grace offers a full pardon for every ounce of that sin. Grace creates fear but then relieves it. Paul asked: 'Or do you presume on the riches of his kindness and forbearance and patience, not knowing that God's kindness is meant to lead you to repentance?' (Romans 2:4). John Newton experienced the precious reception of God's grace as he repented from his many sins.

Newton continued to celebrate with verses declaring God's grace to be an adequate provision for all of the hardships of life. He had complete confidence that the God who had saved him and brought him safely through many dangers, toils and snares would preserve him to the end of life and beyond. This glorious logic is declared in Romans 8:31-32: 'What then shall we say to these things? If God is for us, who can be against us? He who did not spare his own Son but gave him up for us all, how will he not also with him graciously give us all things?' These are 'how much more' questions. If God gave you Jesus to meet your ultimate need of salvation, how much more will he graciously give you everything that you need to cross life's finishing line? God has the power to keep you and then to bring you joyfully into his presence behind the heavenly curtain.

The final verse that Newton wrote is different from the popular finale written by an unknown American poet, which was added to 'Amazing Grace' as early as the mid-nineteenth century. Newton's original finale speaks of the end of this version of the world — the earth dissolving like snow and the sun being snuffed out like a candle. A massive contrast is drawn as the greatest enjoyments of this world will one day come to an end, but our amazingly gracious God will personally be the possession for ever of all believers in the new heaven and the new earth!

God's grace is so great it should take a true believer's breath away! Too often, however, the world clouds our thinking and de-prioritizes the magnitude of gratitude for grace that we should continually express. At the beginning of a brand-new unused year, John Newton considered his past, present and future in the light of God's amazing grace. He called on his church family to do the same. God has repeatedly used Newton's most popular hymn to call his children to do likewise.

'Glorious things of thee are spoken'

The original name of this hymn in *Olney Hymns* was 'Zion, or the City of God'. It was composed for Easter Sunday 1775, and the language is drawn from Isaiah 33 and Psalm 87. In Isaiah 33:20-21 we find these words:

Behold Zion, the city of our appointed feasts!
　　Your eyes will see Jerusalem,
　　an untroubled habitation, an immovable tent,
whose stakes will never be plucked up,
　　nor will any of its cords be broken.
But there the LORD in majesty will be for us
　　a place of broad rivers and streams,
where no galley with oars can go,
　　nor majestic ship can pass.

The sons of Korah begin Psalm 87 with a declaration of glorious blessings of the city of God.

On the holy mount stands the city he founded;
　　the LORD loves the gates of Zion
　　more than all the dwelling places of Jacob.
Glorious things of you are spoken,
　　O city of God

　　　　　　　　　　　　　　　　　　(Psalm 87:1-3).

In the Old Testament, the entire nation of Israel was God's people. Zion, or Jerusalem, was the capital city, and ultimately the location of the tabernacle and later the temple. God was with his special people, manifesting his presence in that special place, in the Holy of Holies above the ark of the covenant. Historically, Jerusalem would have been the greatest place on earth and the safest place for the people of God. After Jesus came, he enlarged the walls of salvation beyond the geographical boundaries of Israel as the gospel was to be proclaimed to the nations. God's people are now comprised of church families of Jews and Gentiles who believe in Jesus in locations all over the earth. The Holy Spirit has been poured out and dwells with his people as spiritual temples wherever they gather. John Newton reads his Old Testament through the prism of Jesus, on this side of the cross. It is right to start with the original context of the Bible wherever you are, but it is also appropriate then to read the parts of the Bible in the light of the whole story.

Newton repaints the glorious image of the city of Zion with all its former blessings as the blessed gathering of the church. Though he starts with the Old Testament pictures, Newton easily alludes to New Testament truths, which are incorporated into his hymn. He inspires believers passionately to ponder the amazing blessings and privileges of being part of the people of God.

The New Testament freely applies the imagery of God's house and God's temple to local churches. Paul called the church the household of God in his first letter to Timothy. 'I hope to come to you soon, but I am writing these things to you so that, if I delay, you may know how one ought to behave in the household of God, which is the church of the living God, a pillar and buttress of the truth' (1 Timothy 3:14, 15). In 1 Corinthians 3:16-17, Paul highlights the significance of the gathered church to warn of the danger of doing harm to the church: 'Do you not know that you are God's temple and that God's Spirit dwells in you? If anyone destroys God's temple, God will destroy him. For God's temple is holy, and you are that temple.' John Newton seems to be on safe ground as he makes the same kinds of heart-felt applications.

Glorious things of thee are spoken,
Zion, city of our God!
He, whose word cannot be broken,
Formed thee for his own abode:
On the rock of ages founded,
What can shake thy sure repose?
With salvation's walls surrounded,
Thou may'st smile at all thy foes.

See! the streams of living waters
Springing from eternal love;
Well supply thy sons and daughters,
And all fear of want remove:
Who can faint while such a river
Ever flows their thirst t'assuage?
Grace, which like the Lord, the giver,
Never fails from age to age.

Round each habitation hov'ring,
See the cloud and fire appear!
For a glory and a cov'ring,
Showing that the Lord is near:
Thus deriving from their banner
Light by night and shade by day;
Safe they feed upon the manna
Which he gives them when they pray.

Blest inhabitants of Zion,
Washed in the Redeemer's blood!
Jesus, whom their souls rely on,
Makes them kings and priests to God:

'Tis his love his people raises
Over self to reign as kings
And as priests his solemn praises
Each for a thank-offering brings.

Saviour, if of Zion's city
I through grace a member am;
Let the world deride or pity,
I will glory in thy name:
Fading is the worldling's pleasure,
All his boasted pomp and show;
Solid joys and lasting treasure,
None but Zion's children know.

Far from just uttering accurate theological statements, John Newton celebrates God's protection and provision in this song, and he motivates his fellow church members to rejoice in the realities expressed as they sing along. Ancient warfare often matched the strength of the defending city's walls and provisions against the endurance of the attackers' siege. Newton makes God's salvation the mighty walls, able to endure the attacks of our serious foes, the world, the flesh, and the devil. As they relentlessly lob flaming arrows of doubt and try to smash the battering ram of accusations against our consciences, we can smile. We have absolutely nothing ultimately to fear. That is the glorious truth!

Newton continues by marvelling at God's never-ending supplies of grace in the second verse. The most essential resource for ancient cities was fresh water. How much more was this the case for desert climates such as Israel! God's people today benefit from something even better than the Gihon spring, Jerusalem's ancient water source; they have the unlimited rivers of God's grace. Those rivers are never diverted. They never dry up. Your soul's thirst can always be quenched.

The song's scene shifts in stanza three from the city to the Sinai desert, where Israel enjoyed the visible symbols of God's protective presence with his people — the glory cloud by day and the pillar of fire by night. Israel was also fed by God himself as the manna fell from heaven. While we do not experience the same tokens God gave Israel, certainly we are blessed with the same benefits of God's protection and provision. Not many of us reside in the desert or even in the modern city of Jerusalem. But Christians are spiritual citizens of Zion, blessed, washed, and relying on Jesus. We are not physical kings and priests, but because of God's grace, we reign over ourselves and sing God's praises with thanksgiving.

Experiencing spiritual citizenship in Zion puts life in proper perspective as the final two verses celebrate. Sometimes we receive sorrows and persecution in the world; at other times the world seeks to lull us into idolatry through pleasure or pumping up our pride. Jesus is a better treasure than anything the world can offer us. Mentally appreciating the surpassing greatness of being united to Jesus is just the start. As our meditations about the exclusive privileges of being a child of Zion fuel our emotions, our whole heart engages and recognizes the solidity of the joys and the eternality of the treasures we have in Jesus. This is the response that syncs our hearts with the reality of God's glory. This makes us sing heartily!

'How sweet the name of Jesus sounds'

Some Christians think of Jesus' name in a magical kind of way. If they merely form the sounds into his name, the devil runs away, all of their problems are solved, and good things drop from the skies into their laps! This is not the point of any of the Bible's references to Jesus' name or any of the best songs about Jesus' name. The literal name of Jesus is the same as the Hebrew name Joshua and was quite common in the Lord's own day. The name of Jesus, however, is the most special name ever. It really is the sweetest word you can ever hear — not because of the combination of letters and sounds, but because it represents all that the Lord Jesus truly is. John Newton wrote a wonderful lyric glorying in the sweetness of Jesus' name, originally titled 'The Name of Jesus' in *Olney Hymns*.

How sweet the name of Jesus sounds
In a believer's ear!
It soothes his sorrows, heals his wounds,
And drives away his fear.

It makes the wounded spirit whole,
And calms the troubled breast;
'Tis manna to the hungry soul,
And to the weary rest.

Dear name! the rock on which I build,
My shield and hiding-place;
My never-failing treas'ry, filled
With boundless stores of grace.

By thee my prayers acceptance gain,
Although with sin defiled,
Satan accuses me in vain,
And I am owned a child.

Jesus! my Shepherd, Husband, Friend,
My Prophet, Priest, and King;
My Lord, my Life, my Way, my End,
Accept the praise I bring.

Weak is the effort of my heart,
And cold my warmest thought;
But when I see thee as thou art,
I'll praise thee as I ought.

Till then I would thy love proclaim
With every fleeting breath,
And may the music of thy name
Refresh my soul in death.

The words of this hymn were inspired by Song of Solomon
1:3: 'your anointing oils are fragrant; your name is oil poured
out; therefore virgins love you.' Other translations compare
the man's name to lovely perfume. John Newton interprets
the Song of Solomon as a love story portraying the relationship between the church and Jesus, so he highlights the sweet
fragrances and healing properties of Jesus' name. But even if
you read Solomon's Song as a literal love story, you can still
marvel at and imitate Newton's love for the Saviour. The content of his lyrics is compiled from all that is revealed about
Jesus throughout the Bible, not simply the Song of Solomon.

Jesus' name stands for all that he is and all that he has done. For a Christian, this becomes deeply personal — it is all that Jesus has done for us. Just as you might consider a cut diamond from various angles, the beautiful refractions of light dancing before your eyes, so also, when you think about Jesus from all kinds of angles, does your heart begin to dance in celebration of his grace? You are filled with faith, joy and satisfaction. When such thoughts are challenged by unbelieving thoughts tempting us to give in to sorrow, pain, and the fears of life, the sweet thought of Jesus wins over our hearts. The great temptation to view life's trials not necessarily in an *anti*-Jesus way but in a *non*-Jesus way is answered by the name of Jesus. The first and second stanzas declare that our spiritual wounds are healed, anxieties are replaced with trust, and spiritual hunger is satisfied.

Newton adds to the encouragement with imagery of security drawn from Psalm 18. Jesus is our rock, shield and hiding-place in verse three. He is also the treasure-chest of grace. Later, in verse five, Newton stacks up a wide array of ways Jesus is revealed to us in the Bible. He is our everything; from husband, to priest, to our very life. Even as a mature Christian minister, Newton never lost sight of the fact that his acceptance before God was because of Jesus' grace, not his own spiritual performance. In verse four, Newton expresses the truth that his access to God was only because of Jesus. The reason for his dependence upon grace is clearly confessed in stanza six: because of the weakness of his spiritual efforts and the coldness of his thoughts. He is prone to become a coal separated from the fire, which changes from red to grey. When Jesus is rightly reoriented in his sight, however, his heart grows warm and rekindles with praise, as the hymn concludes. Newton leads us to keep Jesus' great love flowing from our lips so that we might have persevering faith, spiritually refreshed all the way to death.

'May the grace of Christ our Saviour'

There is a tremendous prayer-wish or benediction tucked into the end of many modern hymnals. John Newton was prompted to write these words by the inspired benediction of 2 Corinthians 13:14: 'The grace of the Lord Jesus Christ and the love of God and the fellowship of the Holy Spirit be with you all.' The source of the blessings is each member of the Trinity — Jesus is sought for his grace, the Father is called upon for his love, and the Holy Spirit's favour for fellowship. The note of grace ripples through each of these blessings.

> May the grace of Christ our Saviour,
> And the Father's boundless love,
> With the Holy Spirit's favour,
> Rest upon us from above!
> Thus may we abide in union
> With each other, and the LORD;
> And possess in sweet communion
> Joys which earth cannot afford.

John Newton had a heart enlarged by gospel grace. He put aside the denominational differences of his day for the gospel. While he always stood for the truth, his fellowship with brothers and sisters was not restricted by his opinions regarding secondary matters. He ended his hymn of benediction singing of the union all true Christians have with one another because of the union each of us has with Jesus Christ. We all have a sweet communion and joy together that the rest of the world cannot even fathom.

The Christian life is much more than just mental assent to a series of facts about Jesus. It is a warm-hearted relationship with a Saviour and Lord. Such affection and adoration must be expressed, and the Lord created music as a vehicle for creatures to make such expressions. The Lord has also raised up gifted men and women to compose lyrics and tunes to help the rest of God's choir members lift their hearts to heaven. The best of these composers, such as John Newton, draw from the richest knowledge of God's Word and widest array of Christian experience to express these wondrous truths passionately in song. John Newton's hymns clearly express his love for the sweet Saviour, and they call other Christians to develop a corresponding love for Jesus!

7

A MAN OF LETTERS

One of the greatest blessings and burdens of life since the mid-1990s is e-mail. How wonderful it is to be able to type out a few lines to a faraway friend and then click 'Send'. Within a flash your friends can see the words of your electronic letter flickering across their computer screens. The cost of these e-letters, clever stories, attached pictures and files (not to mention the advertisements!) is nearly nothing, and the reach of this communication is global through the internet. This happy tool, however, often generates an ominous avalanche of life-clutter. Efficiency experts now add chapters to their books and hours to their seminars just to deal with e-mail's impact on time management!

Although the convenience, speed and affordability of e-mail virtually guarantee its permanent place in our lives, not everything about e-mail is positive when compared to old-fashioned letter-writing. E-mail is both a product of and a contributor to the increasing speed of life. If punctuation, grammar and spelling are victims of the e-mail machine, how much more is attention to the substance of thoughtful content? Personal letters have a legacy of warm expressions and meaningful content. Certainly some letter-writers exhibit much greater skill than others, but I doubt that we will ever see volumes of the collected e-mails of tomorrow's leaders, whereas collections of letters have been helpfully read and passed on for centuries after the authors have died.

John Newton excelled in the art of letter-writing. His endless days at sea while being head over heels in love with Polly drove his pen to pile up pages of pithy love letters. He would write them several days per week and then send the collected bundles when he had the opportunity. Polly would be able to follow large chunks of her husband's adventures at sea as she read the letters in the order in which they were written. God used Newton's long-distance love to sharpen his letter-writing skills for a future mailbox ministry. Newton's pen greatly expanded his pastoral parish.

The best of Newton's spiritual letters were filled with biblical experiential content. But at the same time, they were warm and personal. They took special occasions experienced by the author or recipients and linked the things of real life to Christian living. Because receiving any letter was still quite special in Newton's day, particularly if it was penned by a godly Christian, the author of these letters was aware that they might be read by more people than merely the addressee. In fact, Newton's autobiography about his early life and conversion, *An Authentic Narrative*, began as a collection of letters from John Newton. Even in its expanded published form, the story was still given in the form of letters.

As Newton's faithful ministry grew over the years through his travels and publications, he also enlarged his list of correspondents. By the 1790s, he could have fifty or more letters before him awaiting his reply! Those frustrated today by overcrowded e-mail inboxes can imagine the painful pressure that such expectations of hand-written replies placed on Newton. He once commented that he considered it a tolerably punctual reply if he turned around a letter within six or seven weeks.

But Newton was quite gifted at composing such letters. His pastoral heart, filled with the vast wisdom of years of studying the Scriptures, walking with the Lord Jesus, and shepherding the hearts of his people shines through Newton's engaging correspondence. He freely shares his own Christian and life experiences and adds the light of helpful earthy illustrations as he encourages and interacts with his readers with profound words and big ideas which all neatly fit within the space of his paper.

A consideration of one collection out of his many hundreds of letters offers us a glimpse into John Newton's heart. Themes emerge from his letters which reveal pillars of his understanding of God and man. His ministry style also emerges from these letters, helping us to experience what it would have been like to have John Newton as one's own minister.

In 1780, John Newton published a series of letters under the title of *Cardiphonia*; or, *The Utterance of the Heart, in the Course of a Real Correspondence*. This work, which has been considered Newton's most useful collection of letters, appeared in *The Works of John Newton*, Volumes 1 and 2 (reprinted by The Banner of Truth Trust, Edinburgh, 1988). All of the citations of *Cardiphonia* come from this edition and the page number will follow in parentheses. These private letters which, as was noted, were generally thought of as semi-private in that day, were returned to their author to be compiled and published in book form. These letters were published anonymously, and the identities of the original recipients were hidden. The lion's share of the material was written to 'a Nobleman'. In twenty-six letters to the man later discovered to be the Earl of Dartmouth, his patron at Olney, Newton provided a good return on the investment of the living provided by Lord Dartmouth by offering him encouraging pastoral wisdom and insight. The rest of the collection breaks down into single letters or small series of letters to over twenty other individuals identified only by names such as Mr B., Rev. Mr S., Miss P., and even a Mr ___. After the fact, the identities of both the author and many of the recipients were discovered. The occasions of the letters range widely: from responding to requests for spiritual counsel, to encouraging a fellow pastor, to evangelizing a different pastor, to comforting a widow on the loss of her husband, to encouraging a young Christian girl, and to challenging a young man heading off to university.

John Newton's letters came out of the overflow of his own spiritual journey. In his thirteenth letter to Lord Dartmouth, Newton surmised that ministers (like doctors) were often specialists in different fields of study according to their inclinations and gifts. Newton thought of himself as something of an expert on the human heart. In his autobiography he had traced the responses of his own heart throughout his life. Since his conversion God had been working his amazing grace in and through Newton as a growing Christian husband and then as a Christian minister. During his time in Olney, his study expanded to the hearts of the various characters all about him that he was seeking to serve. He studied their hearts' responses to sin, temptation, affliction, prosperity, sickness, and even the approach of death (1:478). His learning paid rich dividends in his own walk with God as the Lord's streams of grace had made Newton gracious. But he also became an instrument of grace to those to whom he ministered in his letters. Five repeated refrains come up in Newton's letters that form pillars of his pastoral ministry.

1. All things are under the sovereign hand of God

Big things, small things, good things, and even bad things all happen ultimately because of God's sovereign will. This reality gives meaning and purpose to everything that goes on in a person's life. It does not mean that God is responsible for sin in the world. It does not excuse anyone from taking responsibility to honour and obey God with his or her choices. How these apparent contradictions blend together is often beyond human comprehension. That these things are equally and completely true is revealed in the Bible. John Newton believed these things with all his heart. He used this essential understanding that God works his sovereign will through all of life as a tremendous encouragement to those he counselled. Although it did not always explain the hard experiences people endured, believing it and applying it brought perspective and great relief to those to whom Newton ministered. The gap between what a person in crisis can figure out about God's purposes in a given situation and the good purposes that God is actually working out in his or her life is bridged by faith. The person can believe what the Bible says about God's wise plans in spite of what he or she sees and feels.

Reading a history book about the reign of Charles V inspired Newton to write his twenty-sixth letter to the Nobleman, offering him a biblically-informed point of view about history. Exactly one year after the American colonies declared their independence, the pastor from Olney reminded the British nobleman that there is a God in heaven who is sovereign over history, even history in the making!

John Newton describes God's sovereign reign as 'the powerful, though secret, rule of Divine Providence, moving, directing, controlling the designs and actions of men with an unerring hand, to the accomplishment of his own purposes, both of mercy and judgment' (1:552). The world may look like a chaotic mess, but when we unlock the big picture with the key of Scripture, we discover that God is always at work.

In another letter to the same recipient, Newton sought to bolster his reader's theological foundation by declaring,

The government is upon his shoulders; and though he is concealed by a veil of second causes from common eyes, so that they can perceive only the means, instruments, and contingencies by which he works, and therefore think he does nothing; yet, in reality, he does all, according to his own

*counsel and pleasure, in the armies of heaven, and among
the inhabitants of earth*

(1:473).

Later in the letter he also said,

*Before this blessed and only Potentate, all the nations of the
earth are but as the dust upon the balance, and the small
drop of a bucket, and might be thought (if compared with
the immensity of his works) scarcely worthy of his notice:
yet here he presides, pervades, provides, protects, and rules.
In him his creatures live, move, and have their being: from
him is their food and preservation*

(1:474).

Such a great God is worthy of our adoration and is a
trustworthy shelter for every possible storm. In the other
four foundational pillars, we will see Newton weave this
truth in with other kinds of applications. As his friends
suffer through trials, Newton points them to the hands of
his great big God to look for all kinds of benefits that God
is producing through the painful trials. He also sees God as
the essential source for a Christian's dependence. We are
'connected to Infinite Wisdom and Almighty Power. Though
weak as a worm, his arms are strengthened by the mighty
God of Jacob, and all things become possible, yea easy to
him, that occur within the compass of his proper duty and
calling' (1:509).

John Newton's personal dependence on God's sovereign
power in evangelism is evidenced in the way he opened
up the gospel to Thomas Scott, a man who was already a

minister by profession. Newton clearly did not think that the
man was a true believer, and he wisely included the gospel as
he interacted with the substance of the letters which the Rev.
Mr S., as he referred to him in *Cardiphonia*, had written to
him. Notice that, after he tells him of some of the essential
truths of Jesus and the cross, he writes to the man that God
must impart regenerating light to his heart before he will
respond to them. 'Till a person has experienced this change,
he will be at a loss to form a right conception of it: but it
means, not being proselyte to an opinion, but receiving a
principle of Divine life and light in the soul' (1:573). Later
in the same letter, Newton described God's work in saving
a soul.

> And the Spirit of God, by the Gospel, first convinces us of
> unbelief, sin, and misery; and then, by revealing the things of
> Jesus to our minds, enables us, as helpless sinners, to come
> to Christ, to receive him, to behold him, or, in other words, to
> believe in him, and expect pardon, life, and grace from him;
> renouncing every hope and aim in which we once rested,
> 'and accounting all things loss and dung for the excellency of
> the knowledge of Christ'
>
> (1:575).

2. The singular hope of justification by faith alone

Newton asked a question after the massive storm at sea that
he later incorporated into his classic hymn: 'Is God's grace
big enough to save a wretch as bad as me?' His powerful
positive answer became his core conviction and a major
theme of his life and ministry. No matter how wicked a

sinner has been, God can offer him the exchange of the
sinner's wickedness for the righteousness of Jesus, because
of Christ's perfect life, substitutionary death on the cross,
and glorious resurrection.

The cross was the great equalizer for Newton. When a sinner
discovered his sinfulness and felt his need for a Saviour, by
God's grace, the same gift of righteousness was available for
him as Newton had experienced. One time he wrote a letter
describing an opportunity to speak to a group of prisoners.
As he began to share his story, he was surprised at their
attentiveness. He spoke from 1 Timothy 1:15: 'The saying
is trustworthy and deserving of full acceptance, that Christ
Jesus came into the world to save sinners, of whom I am the
foremost.' Newton soberly noted that but for God's grace he
could have easily been in the chains on the other side of the
room. Yet this good message of forgiveness was as much for
them as it had been for him.

He described to a Mrs G. the simple propositions of the
gospel. 'I am a sinner, therefore I need a Saviour, one who
is able and willing to save to the uttermost; such a one is
Jesus: he is all that I want, wisdom, righteousness, sanctifi-
cation, and redemption' (1:681). To the unbelieving pastor,
Thomas Scott, Newton was explicit. He said that the gospel
'speaks to us as condemned already, and calls upon us to believe in a crucified Saviour, that we may receive redemption
through his blood, even the forgiveness of our sins' (1:575).
When Scott wanted to change the subject in another letter,
Newton refocused the conversation on what mattered most,
'the nature of justification, and the method of a sinner's
acceptance with God.' Newton basically called his friend

out as someone who had boasted of his accomplishments. Newton said that he hoped that he would see these religious efforts as Paul saw his — as loss for the sake of Christ, as dung (from Philippians 3:4, 7-10). He wanted Scott to come to spiritual convictions of his total absolute depravity so that every hope and refuge in his own righteousness would be swept away completely and replaced with a real sense of guilt and condemnation. The goal of the awesome experience of conviction would be that Scott would look to Jesus by faith alone and be healed (1:593-594). This was the gospel message that had saved John Newton, and this was the gospel message that Newton preached to everyone he could.

3. The dynamic fight for spiritual growth

Being declared right before God is not the end of the Christian life, but the beginning. God pronounces the sinner righteous as soon as he or she believes in Christ. But the Christian will not actually be perfectly righteous until he or she gets to heaven. The in-between time was where John Newton's special study of the heart was most focused and most refined. His letters include his ideas of the beginning, middle, and mature years of the battles of the Christian for spiritual maturity in this world.

No perfection in this life

John Newton had profound respect for John Wesley. Wesley was a model to Newton of Christian ministry and zeal for the gospel for the people of England from within the Established Church. Wesley was a friend to Newton, offering him personal encouragement and counsel, especially early in his Christian life and ministry. Throughout his life, Newton was known to avoid divisive controversial matters whenever possible. Therefore, it is not hard to imagine the turmoil in Newton's heart as he had to distance himself from Wesley over his Arminianism (that man is ultimately sovereign over his salvation) and particularly his teachings of Perfectionism (that Christians can literally achieve sinless perfection in this lifetime). Although all Christians are free from sin's bondage and powerfully indwelt by the Holy Spirit to pursue holiness, John Newton was convinced by the Scriptures, and by his experience and the experience of every Christian he knew, that Christians will always be marked by battling remaining sin. Newton would go on to say that the more a Christian grows, the more he sees the fight with himself. To the Nobleman he wrote:

> *Far, very far, am I from that unscriptural sentiment of sinless perfection in fallen man. To those who have a due sense of the spirituality and ground of the Divine precepts, and of what passes in their own hearts, there will never be a wanting of cause of humiliation and self-abasement on the account of sin; yet there is a liberty and privilege attainable by the Gospel, beyond what is ordinarily thought of*

(1:454).

Humbling dependence on the Lord

Young believers are full of love and zeal, Newton wrote in his first letter to the noble Lord Dartmouth. They can hardly help preaching to everyone they meet. But one of their biggest dangers is spiritual over-confidence, feeling that they have the Christian life mastered. Newton observes: 'their zeal spends itself in externals and non-essentials' (1:429). He notes that upon discovering the heart-level meaning of the Lord's commands and the weakness in obedience that still exists in the heart of the new Christian, there can be quite a blow of discouragement. But this experiential felt knowledge of remaining sin is an important part of spiritual growth. It creates a profound sense of dependence on the Lord for all spiritual progress.

> By repeated experiments and exercises of this sort (for this wisdom is seldom acquired by one or a few lessons), we begin at length to learn that we are nothing, have nothing, can do nothing but sin. And thus we are gradually prepared to live more out of ourselves, and to derive all our sufficiency of every kind from Jesus, the fountain of grace
>
> (1:430-431).

This sense of the battle with remaining sin, its resulting humility, and the need for complete dependence on Jesus for spiritual strength was absolutely vital from Newton's perspective, and it came up frequently in his letters. To Mr B., Newton compared human nature to soil. Although some soil was better cultivated than others, all of it is universally bad. When Jesus saves a man, it is the husbandman separating some of the soil for himself. He changes it and improves it in every way, but it still retains its propensity to produce weeds. If he stopped weeding the believer, it would revert to a field of weeds again.

> Hence arises the necessity of daily crosses and disappointments, daily changes of frame, and such

> *multiplied convictions, that we are nothing, and can do*
> *nothing, of ourselves; all are needful, and barely sufficient,*
> *to prevent our hearts from being overrun with pride, self-*
> *dependence, and security*
>
> (1:631).

To an apparently youthful believer, My Dear Miss M., the wise minister penned these words about our need for greater spiritual dependence upon the Lord:

> *To make us more sensible of this, he often withdraws*
> *from our perceptions: and as, in the absence of the sun,*
> *the wild beasts of the forest roam abroad; so, when Jesus*
> *hides himself, we presently perceive what is in our hearts,*
> *and what a poor shift we can make without him; when he*
> *returns, his light chases the evils away, and we are well again*
>
> (1:637).

Newton says that without a felt sense of spiritual weakness and dependency, even a professing Christian who starts full of joy and full of zeal for the Lord seldom turns out well. When God shows believers their remaining sin, he works in them 'the savour of brokenness and true humility which is a chief ornament of our holy profession' (1:643).

In his third letter to Mrs G., Newton characterizes the Christian life as reflecting Galatians 5:17, which says: 'For the desires of the flesh are against the Spirit, and the desires of the Spirit are against the flesh, for these are opposed to each other, to keep you from doing the things you want to do.' Yes, a Christian has noble aims, but at every turn we meet the remaining sin which we will not completely shake off until we meet the Lord. The importance of the Christian's knowledge of these realities to Newton can be seen in his own words: 'One eminent branch of our holiness, is a sense of shame and humiliation for those evils which are only known to ourselves, and to him who searches our hearts' (1:690). This sense of our remaining sin humbles us and shames us but should not make us despair. Our Lord Jesus died to rescue us from all of the sins we still see. And he still loves us and will always strengthen us to fight continually against them.

> It is good to be humbled for sin, but not to be discouraged; for though we are poor creatures, Jesus is a complete Saviour; and we bring more honour to God by believing on his name, and trusting his word of promise, than we could do by a thousand outward works

(2:145).

Graciousness built through weakness

Although a Christian is saddened by the discoveries of his consistent spiritual inadequacy within himself, John Newton saw many other virtues that the Lord builds in a humbled child of God. The broken believer is also tenderized by grace. Having to look again and again to Jesus for relational forgiveness and strength to honour him alone builds a tenderness, a willingness, a skill and compassion toward other Christians who are cast down.

> Whoever is truly humbled will not be easily angry, will not be positive and rash, will be compassionate and tender to the infirmities of his fellow-sinners, knowing, that, if there be a

difference, it is grace that has made it, and that he has the
seeds of every evil in his own heart

(1:452).

Newton was known by all parties as a gospel man and a gospel minister. While some segments of the church build high walls to protect themselves and their flocks from doctrinal differences even on secondary and tertiary matters, and seek to fashion the kingdom along the political lines of their own denomination, John Newton, the Anglican, cultivated warm and lasting friendships with all fellow gospel men and women. He regularly scandalized those from his own denomination (even some within Polly's family!), by being so friendly to the Baptists, Methodists and Independents. Part of John Newton's gospel catholicity sprang from this gospel tenderization. He had a great sense of his personal inadequacy and Christ's amazing patience and grace to him: how could he not extend those same virtues to others, especially towards those that he was confident proclaimed the same gospel as himself?

The world is a spiritual battlefield

In addition to the battles believers face from within their own remaining sinful flesh, John Newton never lost sight of the spiritual enemies constantly working against Christians. He regularly reminded the recipients of his letters to be alert for adversaries. He put examples of this danger before the Nobleman in his twenty-third letter to him. David and Hezekiah were both godly kings of Israel who both experienced tragic spiritual failures before they finished their missions. Newton wanted the godly Nobleman to take heed for himself.

> *But by temptation we more frequently understand the wiles and force which Satan employs in assaulting our peace, or spreading snares for our feet. He is always practicing against us, either directly from himself, by the access he has to our hearts, or mediately, by the influence he has over the men and the things of this world*
>
> (1:525-526).

Newton renders the supplication in the Lord's prayer, 'Lead us not into temptation, but deliver us from *the evil one*', as more evidence of the need for dependence upon the Lord for spiritual victory. Without the Lord, our cause would be hopeless against such a strong and tireless foe, but because of the Lord's protection we have hope for safety (1:526).

The devil and his demons, according to Newton, wage war against every aspect of a Christian's life: his understanding, by blinding the mind with false reasoning and arguments that lead to erroneous conclusions; his conscience, using unbelief to cloud the glories of the gospel; his will, by pressing his weak flesh to choose to disobey God; his affections, by infecting them with a love for the things of this world; his imagination, sometimes being permitted to tyrannize people so that they wildly concoct all kinds of vain lines of thought (1:526-531). Satan subtly uses good things, dear friends, and even God's blessings as snares to lead us to gaze upon the gifts and away from God, the giver.

John Newton looked behind influential thinkers of his day who were trying to rationally promote atheism and saw Satan's dark inspiration.

After making the best allowances I can, both for the extent
of human genius, and the deplorable evil of the human heart,
I cannot suppose that one half of the wicked wit, of which
some persons are so proud, is properly their own. Perhaps
such a one as Voltaire would neither have written, nor
have been read or admired so much, if he had not been the
amanuensis of an abler hand in his own way. Satan is always
near, when the heart is disposed to receive him ... assisting
[the sinner] with such strokes of blasphemy, malice, and
falsehood, as perhaps he could not otherwise have attained
                                                        (1:490).

Just two months into the war over the American colonies
which had declared independence from British rule, Newton
had war on his mind in a fifth letter to Mr B. A young
Christian woman they both knew had been battling a severe
sickness for a while. She was quite weak. Newton identifies
the spiritual battle going on beyond the physical battle. 'The
enemy, who always fights against the peace of the Lord's
children, finds great advantage against them when their
spirits are weakened and worn down by long illness, and is
often permitted to assault them' (1:627). The Lord permits
these trials for wise and ultimately good purposes, but that
does not always relieve the immediate struggle. Newton
goes on in the letter to declare:

Believers are soldiers: all soldiers by their profession are
engaged to fight, if called upon; but who shall be called to
sustain the hottest service, and be most frequently exposed
to the field of battle, depends on the will of the general
or king. Some of our soldiers are now upon hard service in

*America, while others are stationed around the palace, see
the king's face daily, and have no dangers or hardships to
encounter*

(1:627).

The benefits of adversity

Suffering is a major tool that the Lord Jesus uses for the
spiritual maturity of his children. Although the final
product is so valuable to those experiencing the trials, the
process is often overwhelming. Suffering saints often look
to spiritual leaders for comfort in these painful tribulations.
As a beloved minister in the quaint English town of Olney,
John Newton did not consider himself to have had much
adversity in his Christian life, but the Lord gave him a large
pastor's heart of mercy for those in his ministry who had
suffered much. He considered helping those enduring trials
to be a major part of his preaching and personal ministry
(2:22). One of Newton's strategies in comforting the afflicted
was to highlight the blessings God builds into the hearts of
his suffering children.

Some of the advantages of afflictions that Pastor Newton
tenderly pens for different suffering readers are as follows:

1. It motivates them to pray;
2. It redirects the sufferer's love from the world to heaven;
3. God's Word comes to life experientially;
4. God's grace is evidenced to the one suffering and to
    those around him or her;
5. Personal spiritual graces are strengthened by use;
6. Christlikeness is formed;

7. It proves adoption by God;
8. It reveals the corruption of the heart;
9. It develops tenderness and skill in ministering to others
    in trials;
10. Opportunities are provided to witness to the truthfulness,
    power and sweetness of God's promises;
11. It provides a training ground for gospel service;
12. It uproots deep pride;
13. Satisfaction with this world is severed and a heart for
    heaven is produced.

In his seventh letter to the anonymous recipient, Newton
recounted a visit to a mutual acquaintance in an asylum.
After mentioning his gratitude for being in his right senses
and not being in hell or in a place like Bedlam, Newton
reflected on the Lord's dealings with his people.

> The Lord afflicts us at times: but it is always a thousand times
> less than we deserve, and much less than many of our fellow-
> creatures are suffering around us. Let us therefore pray for
> grace to be humble, thankful, and patient
>
> (2:151).

Newton's illustrations of the sea seem authentic enough for
the reader to taste salt in the air. He compared our hope in
the Lord through stormy trials in his first letter to Mr C.:

> We sail upon a turbulent and tumultuous sea; but we are
> embarked on a good [boat], and in a good cause, and we
> have an infallible and almighty Pilot, who has the winds
> and weather at his command, and can silence the storm
> into a calm with a word whenever he pleases. We may be

persecuted, but we shall not be forsaken; we may be cast
down, but we cannot be destroyed. Many will thrust sore at
us that we may fail, but the Lord will be our stay

(2:155).

4. Motivation of gospel grace

The gospel is for Christians. Certainly all true Christians
recognize that the message that — through Jesus and his
work on the cross — God can justly declare the believing
sinner to be righteous is great news for unbelievers. But
that same message is important for believers as well. The
fact that we are initially saved through faith alone and
not by religious works does not stop us being tempted to
assume that those same religious works keep us saved, or
at least add to God's good opinion of us (or that our lack
of them will ruin our right standing in heaven!). This kind
of performance thinking about a Christian's relationship
with God represents a lack of proper gospel orientation.
When Christians remind themselves that their perfectly
right standing with God is ever and only based upon Jesus
and his work on the cross, a dramatic heart change occurs.
The gospel humbles us, makes us more dependent on Jesus
alone, fills our heart with gratitude and fresh love for the
Lord, and motivates us to honour the Lord with sustained
obedience to his commands.

Although the New Testament may not use modern Christian
catch-phrases, the writers bring up the work of Christ and
the Christian's position united to Christ so often in the
letters written to established believers and churches that

it should not come as a shock to think that the gospel is a critical component in spiritual growth. Bible students have long noted that the indicatives (statements of facts) precede the imperatives (the commands for Christians to obey). Throughout the history of the church, Christian leaders and pastors have spoken of gospel motivation for Christian obedience. The man amazed by God's grace, John Newton, both experienced that motivation and put it before those to whom he ministered.

In his fourth letter to Lord Dartmouth, John Newton wrote:

> *The more vile we are in our own eyes, the more precious he will be to us; and a deep repeated sense of the evil in our hearts is necessary to preclude all boasting, and to make us willing to give the whole glory of our salvation where it is due*
> (1:444).

Newton moves from prizing the one who saved us to the solid motivation produced by the gospel in his fourteenth letter to the same recipient.

> *To know that he loved us, and gave himself for us, is the constraining argument and motive to love him, and surrender ourselves to him; to consider ourselves as no longer our own, but to devote ourselves, with every faculty, power, and talent, to his service and glory. He deserves our all; for he parted with all for us*
> (1:486).

It is sad to feel our sinful inadequacy, but it is sweet to see that God's grace is greater than our greatest sins. That grace

is not idle — it stirs us to activity. In his first letter to a
completely anonymous person Newton said,

> *Wait on the Lord, and he will enable you to see more and
> more of the power and grace of our High Priest. The more
> you know him, the better you will trust him: the more you
> trust him, the better you will love him; the more you love
> him, the better you will serve him*

(2:141).

John Newton pointed those to whom he wrote to the means
of grace that God uses to awaken and keep their hearts
engaged and energized for godliness. When Miss F. asked
for counsel about staying near the Lord and away from the
world, Newton pointed her to these wonderful means. He
called her to pray. He specified, 'above all things, we should
pray for humility. It may be called both the guard of all other
graces, and the soil in which they grow.' He also pointed her
to the Bible, highlighting its promises, its examples, and the
clear revelation of 'the whole scheme of Gospel salvation.'
Finally, Newton called this young Christian lady to vigilance
— being watchful against any temptations to which she was
particularly vulnerable (1:694-695).

As he included himself in his encouragement to a fellow
minister, the Rev. Mr B., John Newton's perspective on
the treasure-chest that the Word of God is for all believers
becomes abundantly plain:

> *But, above all, may we, dear sir, live and feed upon the
> precious promises, John xiv. 16, 17, 26; and xvi.13–15. There is
> no teacher like Jesus, who by his Holy Spirit reveals himself in*

his word to the understanding and affections of his children.
When we thus behold his glory in the Gospel glass, we are
changed into the same image. Then our hearts melt, our
eyes flow, our stammering tongues are unloosed

(2:99).

5. Aiming towards heaven

It is natural to live in the light of what a person sees and experiences all around themselves. As fish are only oriented to
the lake in which they live, so humans are naturally oriented to swim among the things of our world. But God has put
eternity in our hearts. The Christian, especially the Christian
minister, must live and minister in this world in the light of the
world to come. Heaven changes everything. All that heaven
stands for is what changes things right here and now. As John
Newton walked the streets of Olney, he did not just see lace-
makers trying to earn a little pittance to subsist upon, he saw
people who would live for eternity. The struggles of this life
are preparations for the life to come. Wrongs done against
them would certainly be righted. The best things they experienced in their simple lives were tokens of the glories
that follow death. These people would one day meet Jesus
— that much was certain. The question before John Newton
was whether they would meet Jesus as their Saviour or their
Judge. Having an eye on heaven affected the way Newton
ministered as a local pastor and through his wise letters.

Newton tried to encourage his Nobleman friend by elevating
his thoughts to the world to come. Newton encouraged him
always to fill his heart with the reality of the glorious day that

eternity begins. He counselled him to 'estimate all things around us *now*, by the view in which they will appear to us *then*' (1:470). The small but faithful people in this world may be the princes of the next, while today's rich and powerful may be doomed as they face the judgement. He reminded the Nobleman to live this life in the light of eternity and commended him for doing so.

Thinking about the end times ought not to be a mere curiosity or an enjoyable diversion from real life; eternity should affect how we handle temporal things. Newton wished that the 'cheering contemplation of the hope set before us, support and animate us to improve the interval, and fill us with an holy ambition of shining as lights in the world, to the praise and glory of his grace, who has called us out of darkness' (1:471-472). Thoughts of Jesus, his righteousness, our final righteousness, and that holy place of happiness for ever should saturate our souls with joy and hope. Our priorities should shift to the things that matter most, and energize us to honour the Lord with all our might. Thank heaven for thoughts of heaven!

As important as thoughts of heaven must be for believers, Christians are not naturally fond of thinking about death and eternity. God helps his children think of the world to come in various ways. Newton once observed that one reason that God allows believers to continue in sinful ways is to weary us from the fight and to make us long for that final place of eternal victory perhaps more than anything else:

> Death is unwelcome to nature; — but then, and not till then, the conflict will cease. Then we shall sin no more. The flesh,

with all its attendant evils, will be laid in the grave. Then the
soul, which has been partaker of a new and heavenly birth,
shall be freed from every incumbrance, and stand perfect in
the Redeemer's righteousness before God in glory

(1:436).

In addition to the fatigue of fighting with sin, Newton believed the effects of old age and the accumulated impact of the trials of life were designed by God to lift our hearts to heaven. He once concluded a second letter to the Rev. Mr R. with the outstanding contrast of eternal heaven to the few and evil days of this vain world. 'Sin has so envenomed the soil of this earth, that the amaranth [an ornamental flower] will not grow upon it. But we are hasting to a better world, and bright unclouded skies, where our sun will go down no more, and all tears shall be wiped from our eyes' (1:652-653). In the next letter to the same minister, Newton's eternal perspective helped him relate to the toughest times in this world. 'A few years will set all to rights; and they who love him and are beloved by him, though they may suffer as others, shall not sorrow as others; for the Lord will be with them here, and he will soon have them with him: there all tears shall be wiped from their eyes' (1:655).

John Newton's heart as a pastor shines through what he did with his pen. Instead of trying to avoid correspondence for the sake of the ministry, he determined that letter-writing was a significant part of that ministry. He effectively crafted thoughtful, biblical pages, wisely guiding people from all stations of life through all situations of life. The old sea captain helped many saints sail through the storms of this life and prepare for the eternal harbour of heaven.

Recommendations for Further Reading

Jonathan Aitken, *John Newton: From Disgrace to Amazing Grace* (Wheaton, IL: Crossway Books, 2007).

This splendid biography builds on previous works and thorough research. It moves like an action-packed adventure story.

Todd Murray, *Beyond Amazing Grace* (Darlington: Evangelical Press, 2007).

This anthology of John Newton weaves the author's heart-felt devotional interaction with wonderful quotations from John Newton's hymns, sermons and letters arranged topically. It is wonderful devotionally and historically.

Richard Cecil, *The Life of John Newton*, ed. Marylynn Rouse (Fearn, Ross-shire: Christian Focus, 2000).

> *As a contemporary of John Newton, Cecil writes Newton's story with authority. The aged Newton personally read with approval much of the manuscript. In this edition, Marylynn Rouse has added the treasures of her tireless research to the original biography, making the appendices and footnotes every bit as valuable as the body of the work. The Who's Who appendix gives a summary of all the major figures who intersected with Newton.*

Bruce Hindmarsh, *John Newton and the English Evangelical Tradition* (Grand Rapids, MI: Eerdmans, 1996).

> *This major work thoroughly fills out the evangelical background of John Newton's day.*

Bruce Hindmarsh, *The Spirituality of John Newton* (Vancouver: Regent College Publishing, 1998).

> *This work includes a very nice essay by the author introducing his critical edition of John Newton's* An Authentic Narrative *and three letters from Newton's* Omicron *on growing in spiritual maturity.*

John Newton, *Select Letters of John Newton* (Edinburgh: Banner of Truth Trust, reprinted 2012).

> *This selection contains thirty-nine practical letters on a variety of subjects.*

John Newton (updated and revised by Dennis R. Hillman), *Out of the Depths* (Grand Rapids, MI: Kregel, 2003).

This is a modernized version of Newton's autobiography.